MIRACLE KID

MIRACLE KID

The Seventeen-Year-Old Newborn

THE TRUE STORY OF ZACHARY D. GAUVIN

BY

ZACHARY D. GAUVIN

"You can only look in one direction; forward . . . looking at
the past can only hold you back from accomplishing your
Goals in the future . . ."

-Zachary D. Gauvin

iUniverse, Inc.
Bloomington

MIRACLE KID
The Seventeen-Year-Old Newborn

iUniverse books may be ordered through booksellers or by contacting:

iUniverse
1663 Liberty Drive
Bloomington, IN 47403
www.iuniverse.com
1-800-Authors (1-800-288-4677)

Because of the dynamic nature of the Internet, any web addresses or links contained in this book may have changed since publication and may no longer be valid. The views expressed in this work are solely those of the author and do not necessarily reflect the views of the publisher, and the publisher hereby disclaims any responsibility for them.

Any people depicted in stock imagery provided by Thinkstock are models, and such images are being used for illustrative purposes only.
Certain stock imagery © Thinkstock.

Cover Image belongs to Sentinel & Enterprise Newspaper

ISBN: 978-1-4697-8637-7 (sc)
ISBN: 978-1-4697-8639-1 (hc)
ISBN: 978-1-4697-8638-4 (ebk)

Library of Congress Control Number: 2012903439

Printed in the United States of America

iUniverse rev. date: 02/21/2012

DEDICATION

My Family
Community of Leominster, MA

TABLE OF CONTENTS

INTRODUCTION

I may sound confused in some of the chapters throughout this book. This is not only because of my brain injury and I my real confusion, but also because much of this was journaling . . . I wrote what I was feeling and thinking in the moment. I would sometimes forget what I said in a previous chapter or what I was feeling, which would led me to repeat or contradict myself. I simply let the emotions I had build up inside and I'd sit to write.

One of the messages of my book is patience, which I learned very well during to the accident. Life requires patience because life takes time to sort itself out, especially when letting the brain heal. You do not get the fast results you think you'll get. There are two goals I had writing this book; one is to help people not take life for granted because every day is a blessing, the other is to describe the physical and mental aspects of recovering from a traumatic brain injury. Everyone can see the physical stress a trauma patient goes through, but no one can know the mental torment I went through trying to piece my life back together. I also wrote this book to give fellow survivors a luxury I never had; the luxury of knowing what to expect. I wanted to give a firsthand account of recovering from a brain injury and to let them know they are not alone.

First I WOULD JUST LIKE TO SAY

Thank you Lord for keeping me alive . . . who ever put me through this I almost want to thank them. I know it sounds weird but I can truly appreciate everything in life especially the small things, now . . . thank you Lord . . .

I was a sophomore in college when I put this in my AIM profile and my mother said she liked it a lot. I wanted to share with you how I felt when I finally realized this was a blessing in disguise.

First, the seventeen year-old newborn means . . . yes, I did get another chance at life and literally having to learn life all over again.

I am writing this because I want people to know what it is like to have everything you could ever want and yet make one bad decision and have it all taken away. I also wanted to write this book for everyone who takes life for granted, whether playing a sport or just performing an everyday activity such as walking or running. Every day you make it through is a blessing in and of itself. You should wake in the morning and thank God that you get one more day to walk the Earth. I was absolutely miserable when I started writing this book. I couldn't do anything. I hated going to bed because I knew that I would have to wake up in the morning and be the person I hated having become.

I hope I can help doctors and people dealing with a brain injury. No one should have to experience what I have had to endure. I am not saying that to sound sentimental, but the mental torment was such a burden aside from all the physical recovery I went through. I hope with this book I am able to help doctors and psychologist help assist patients with brain injuries. When I went through my rehab I was completely lost. I had no one to turn to. No one could relate. There is no medical explanation as to why I am alive or why I can do all I can do. But if I can help one person with this book, then I believe I found my reason for still being here.

PREFACE

S ome of the names in this book have been changed in order to keep their identity private.

Finally. Freshman year of high school. I have waited my whole life for this. This was going to be the best time of my life and define who I would become. I was so excited for my first day of high school. I had all my dreams and goals planned. I already knew what I wanted to accomplish duringmy tenure at Leominster High School. I was going to be captain of the varsity football team, and I would start on varsity as a junior. And as for baseball I was going to start at least one game as a freshman on varsity. I had aspirations to hit near .500 and play division one baseball then get drafted. It may sound funny, but this is what I wanted from the first time I picked up a bat. I was two and my dad would throw baseballs to me. So, I played freshman football and was a captain. But sooner than expected it was baseball season. I was asked to play on the junior varsity team as a freshman. I batted .750 and got the call up to varsity. I started one game and made the team when the roster expanded for playoffs. Babe Ruth all-stars. I hit just over .500. One of the best summers of my life playing ball.

In my sophomore year, my best friend was named Natasha. And I thought she was the one for me. because the only problem was she had a boyfriend, I had a girl friend, and we were after all, best friends. But, I still knew something special was between us. After all I won homecoming king, I was the stud of the sophomore class, what girl wouldn't want me, right?

I made football captain and I played wide receiver and free safety on the JV team. We had one play where the quarterback would throw the ball to me as I ran wide. Then I would throw it to another receiver. Well, around 75% of the time we got a touchdown on this play. One time we were playing Brockton and ran this play and I released the ball and I got hit so hard my helmet flew into the air. I bleed profusely from my chin. There was blood everywhere. I had to get stitches on my chin near my throat. I was worried that because I could not play for a couple of days I would lose my spot as a starter. When I was healthy I fell right into the spot like nothing had happened.

My girlfriend Toni, and I only lasted a year. Late into that football season she got drunk at a party and cheated on me with one of my good friends. I was heartbroken and all my friends were mad. So Derek, the quarterback of the varsity team who became my best friend, my brother, over the football season, said to me "Come on. Let's go. We're going to forget all about her." He took me to my first party with the junior and senior guys from the football team. This is where my drinking habit developed.

The following winter was one party after another. I drank in the morning before school after school, week nights, by myself and every weekend. There were times I broke into people's homes because I was too drunk to realize it was not where the party was. I slept in the trunks of friends' cars (do you have any idea how scary it is to wake up in a trunk?). I had no regard for my body or other people's property. But if you had met me you would have never known. I was a very respectful kid who was completely normal. Get a couple of drinks in me and I didn't have a care in the world.

This drinking problem began to affect my baseball game. I would go out and drink the night before a game. I remember playing games still drunk from the night before. I still held a respectable .321 average at the plate, and was one of the best clutch hitters in the county. My glove was much better than my hitting as I could make catches that seemed impossible. Even my coach who never gives a compliment and was 70 years old, told me I had made one of the best catches he had ever seen. Only a sophomore, I took the city of Leominster's baseball by force. So cool and calm when I got up to the dish to hit and in the outfield I looked like I was twelve years old again. I would run around the outfield shagging fly balls with a huge smile on my face. I had no worries. I just did what

I had always done; having a blast while doing something I loved. One evening, I got the phone call. It was Coach Rafuse, or Sid who coached the local American Legion team, who I had known forever. He taught me the game and the fundamentals of baseball since I was very young. My little brother Mike and I would always be in attendance at the clinics he held. For a few days we played a cat and mouse game of phone tag. I still remembered what he said exactly when I finally got in touch with him. "So you with us?" and I exclaimed "Yes" ecstatically.

Legion post 151. The best time of my life playing baseball. We were so good. Our team was comprised of kids in college and kids from all over the county. I was only a sophomore, but got sufficient playing time. Andrew Hudson (another sophomore) and I played a frequently. We were something special. It's kind of ironic that later we would be the ones unable to play senior year and most of junior year. The Legion team was awesome. The level of baseball was amazing. They were the elite at this age, and I was here playing with them. I learned so much watching the older players. This experience made me a better player even if I didn't get to start many games.

I drank all the way through and after my Legion season. During the summer, immediately following my Legion season, my three friends and I drank a whole handle of Jim Bean whisky in 45 minutes. I remember vague groggy details of sitting in a car as my friend drove us to the store then everything goes black. I cannot tell you anything that happened that night except my face hurt extremely bad because my head hit the trash can while I was throwing up. The worst part is that I attempted to go swimming and almost drowned. My friend had to rescue my floating body from the water.

Football my jounior year. This year I would get a decent amount of playing time on varsity and if it was up to me I would start. I spent the whole summer when I wasn't drinking training for my opportunity to get a starting position. Summer camp came for football and I was a lock for starting cornerback. I would also see time at wide-receiver as a flanker, or so I thought. The first game night was against Everette High School, and the first D went onto the field. I did not get the start. My friend Tony did. I was happy for him, but I couldn't believe I wasn't starting. I followed coach around as if I were an annoying rectal itch. My time came when Tony made a fatal mistake that gave the other team a first down. Pissed, Coach yelled "GAUVIN! Go get him out." I never looked back. The job was mine and I was not going to give it back. I got five interceptions on the year and scored a touchdown on one. My picture was in the paper it seemed every weekend. I was truly living the dream. The parties were awesome, football was going great, grades were good, and the girls . . . well, girls couldn't have been any better. Natasha was the homecoming queen for the junior class, and she was wore my #24 jersey. I used to think to myself "Wow, just like the movies the prettiest girl in the school is wearing my jersey and wanted to date me." We were so good that our team went to the high school super bowl to play Long Meadow who hadn't lost in years. We played our balls off, but our Coach at one point during the game made a choice to attempt a two-point conversion; we did not get it and lost by one point: 21-20.

I asked Natasha to be my girlfriend Christmas of 2005. I went to Build-a-Bear and designed a bear in a tuxedo. I voice recorded myself so that when you squeezed the hand of the bear it said, "Natasha, will you be my girlfriend." She jumped up and down freaking out so much she didn't even hear the question. I had to replay it for her when she calmed and then she exclaimed "Yes!"

Winter set in and I was a full-on alcoholic. There was no hiding it. I had a drinking problem and the worst part of my problem was that I liked to drive when I drank. I thought I was the best drunk driver ever. I remember there were times I would drive on the highway and all my friends would be in the car cheering me on. "Go Faster, Zach!" so I did.

"How fast you think I can get it to go before the governor chip kicks in?"

I was an idiot. I did . . . . 115 mph once. I was drunk, and drunk to me in high school meant absolutely wasted. There were times I threw up inside my car as I drove it. Disgusting, right? Well, to me this was considered a fun weekend.

My best high school memory came when I was sober. It was a February night in Massachusetts and I could see my warm breath cut through the cold air. I was crouched behind a bush waiting for my brother to get home. I was dressed ridiculously with a black wet suit on and women's nylons pulled over my face. My brother's girlfriend's Jeep pulled up. His girlfriend was aware of what was about to transpire and ran into the house. My brother and his friend Dave got out of the car throwing eggs in every direction. Fifteen of my friends came out of the woods and ran straight for them. I, being the leader, tackled my brother. As my friend Matt pulled his white van with no windows up to the curb, I jumped into the van with my brother in a firm headlock. Crack! Ooze dripped down my face. My brother had just cracked his last egg on my head and now I had egg goo caught in the nylons. The plan was to take my brother up to the little league field near my house so we could torment him, as a joke.

When we got there I got this great idea to strip my brother and his friend down to their boxers. The next step was to tie them to the fence. This failed miserably because my brother took off running and he is extremely fast. My friend Travis busted his ass on a thin layer of ice after he hurdled a fence in pursuit. We finally corralled my brother. Someone held him and his friend to prevent them from running off and I proceeded to slap them in the face with raw steaks. The juicy pieces of meat made a wonderful slapping sound as I smacked my brother and his friend in the face. It was all fun and games until my dad came to the field. He thought I had hurt my brother. He asked me repeatedly, yelling at me asking if I'd hurt him. Everyone including my brother yelled "No!" When my dad got angry or mad it was best to step out of the way. I don't remember exactly what happened but my dada grabbed me by the shirt and my face ended up hitting the van window and my eye swelled up so big that I couldn't see out of it. I called this procedure "Operation Badaday," which is a word I found in the urban dictionary.

To play Div I baseball, I had to get some exposure. I asked my friend who was getting recruited by division one schools how to get noticed. He told me one of the best ideas was go to a clinic/showcase at Northeastern University in Boston. I decided to give it a try. The moment I took my first cut, coaches surrounded me to watch. I had lightening quick hands and the coaches loved this. I was hoping this would give me the edge over the bigger kids because when a 92-mph fastball rides high and tight all they could try to do is muscle a blooper over the infielder's heads, if that. All the other kids there were much, much bigger than I.

Varsity baseball as a junior—could not have gone any better. I was the starting center fielder for the varsity team and batted second. No one could bunt like I could and that's why I batted second.

My Coach's 600th win—we were playing a Worcester team and it came down to one run. The baseball God's called on me and I answered. I roped a single right over the first basemen's head. I knocked in the winning run, the runner was my friend "Q" who, jumped up and down to celebrate. I ran around all the bases as fast as I could I was thinking triple easy. Too bad the game was over and it didn't matter. I looked like such an ass. After the game I was interviewed by Fox 25 news.

I was batting just over .500 The day everything changed for me, the night I was steps from death, I went 0-4 and my average plummeted to .466.

I was the kid who would lead the prayer for the football team the Thursday before every game. I was voted captain for my senior year in football and voted captain for my senior year in baseball I hit the game winner in my coach's 600th win, I was going to play division 1 baseball, my grades were good, I had the best looking girl in the school, teachers and students loved me, and I was in the best shape of my life. I was just a good kid, who did stupid things.

CHAPTER 1

TBI

I wake up in a room that is strange to me. Everything in my mind is groggy, my eyes aren't focusing, and nothing makes sense. I search for my mother who I can hear crying profusely. I looked around the room trying to make sense of the noises and bodies around me. My friends, and family, all looked as sad as I'd ever seen them. This was just another day, right? Morning. I'd woken from a night of sleep into this awkward moment. But if it was just another day, why were they all here staring at me? I keep scanning the room trying to make sense of it all. I had tubes everywhere. There's one, there's another, there's one going into my stomach filled with some sort of brown liquid.

This is right around the time where I start to believe I have just woken at my friend's beach house in Maine. For whatever reason, there really is no rational explanation; I simply thought I had woken in Maine. And with this thought, more questions flood my mind. How did I get in Maine? Yesterday I was home in Leominster, Mass. Today I'm in Maine? Why is my mother in Maine, sitting by the window crying?

Then the peculiar hallucinations. I can feel the bed trying to suck me in, almost as if it was eating me alive. The harder I try to free myself from the evil hunger of the bed, the more it sucks me in. I am sick of being in this bed and I want out. Every time I try to get out, I can't. The whole left side of my body will not cooperate, as if the left side is not receiving signals from my brain to move.

I start to yell and scream. I'm yelling for help from everyone in the room, but for some reason they do not help. I yell and yell and yell.

They don't seem to see me lying here, being devoured, screaming for their attention. No one answers my call. It is as almost like they cannot understand what I am saying. My mouth is hard to open; it feels like something is restricting it from opening wide or at all.

Then a friend came to my side and began removing all tubes penetrating my body. I yell his name, Gonzo! Gonzo! Gonzo! But he does not understand. What's worse, it seems he didn't even hear me. Then I realize this man looks nothing like my friend Gonzo. *Wait, this isn't Gonzo, who is this man?* I soon realize that he is a doctor.

My usual schedule is that I wake up every day and go to the gym at five, right before school. This way I can get the gym out of the way and not have to go in the evening. I would get out of practice at six in the evening with ample time to hang out with my girlfriend before too late at night. Time with her was valuable, every moment counted, because I had to work so hard to get her to go out with me (but that's another story for later). I was currently batting .466 on a high school baseball team. With my hard work, disciplined schedule, I believed my dream would come true. I was going to go to a division one school to play baseball. But these doctors and these tubes and the fact that I feel I'm in Maine creates a panic in me. This isn't my routine. This isn't a part of my path to success.

Fellow doctors run into the room and they tell me that they are going to prepare me for transportation. *Transportation? Where?* They picked me up and placed me on a bed with wheels. They picked me up almost the same way you would pick up a small child and throw him in the pool. One man grabbed my legs and another grabbed my armpits. Confused, but ecstatic for escaping the jaws of that evil bed, I lay and ponder the places they could be taking me.

I fell asleep shortly after and woke up in an ambulance on my way to Spaulding Rehab in Boston. My mother sat next to me in the ambulance. She began to tell me a story as foreign to me as the scene I'd just woken up in. She said, "You were involved in a serious car accident. You have been in a coma for a month." The message meant almost nothing to me. I was still relaxed from morphine running through my veins. None of the words she spoke seemed real. "We are on our way to Boston, where you will have rehab." *Rehab, ya right I'm in the best shape of my life. I'm captain of the football team, going to be captain of the baseball team.* She continued, "The doctors said you must relearn how to do everything all over again." Though I still couldn't realize it at that exact moment, everything I had ever worked for had come crashing down. All the physical attributes, the baseball skills, the hours in the gym over the years were all now irrelevant.

Mom told me I had sustained a Traumatic Brain Injury and that I had injured the right side of my brain so badly that I had what is called left side neglect. This meant that my entire left side, though intact and normal appearing, was uncontrollable. I could not move or connect with it. I remember lying in my bed, looking at my hands and trying to make them move, and nothing would happen with my left hand or arm. I could move my right one just fine. But I would try to move them simultaneously, and my left hand remained flat.

She told me that I had broken my jaw and had to have my jaw wired shut. It all began to make sense. *That's why no one could understand me when I tried to talk.* I had rubber bands that ran up and down my mouth, vertically, to restrict my mouth from opening too far. She told me to induce me in the coma the doctors had given an overdose of morphine. For a month I laid in bed with an overdose of morphine running through my veins to keep me comatose.

My mother started to list off all the injuries I received when my 2002 Chevy Blazer veered off the highway and rolled over several times. I only remember the night it happened from stories friends told me. I went 0-4 in a baseball game that morning. Though I was still batting a hot .466 for the season, going hitless haunted me all day. I needed to get the game off my mind. I went to a barbeque with the person who meant the most to me at that time, Natasha, my girlfriend. There was drinking at this barbeque, but I didn't drink much as I had to go to a college baseball game later in the day. I wanted to watch two teams that I could possibly play for next year in college, Holy Cross and the University of Rhode Island.

My friend T.J. and I went to the game for only a little while. URI was killing Holy cross. We left and headed home. I had plans with Natasha, but she instead decided to make plans with her girl-friends. So T.J. and I decided to attend a party. We pre-gamed (played drinking games) at a friend's house before the real party began.

We arrive at the party, Natasha's ex-boyfriend was there. This I believe made me drink more. I couldn't let Natasha's ex show me up, right? So I ended up drinking too much. He started feeding me shots one by one and, I being the "champ" I was would not back down from the challenge. No surprise, and to the point, I was absolutely trashed. I blacked out completely. From that moment on, even without the accident, I wouldn't remember the next several hours. My friends said I was completely blitzed.

I took the keys and ran from my friend who held them. I was going to meet T.J back at his house and stay for the night. We took the highway like always, me leading T.J. who followed. My car veered to the side of the road and according to the police report dropped off the shoulder, struck the end of the guardrail. After Impact, the car began to rotate clockwise for approximately seventy-six feet. Next, the left rear door struck one of the support posts for an advertising sign. It rolled numerous times smashing my head around the car.

My parents say that miraculously I was able to get out of the car and walk to the other side. I proceeded to the other side of the car and fell into a pile of leaves where I was found. We like to believe that Dante (my grandfather who had passed several years ago) came down from heaven and assisted me; I always believed he was my guardian angel. But Trooper Dwyer who found me said I didn't walk at all. I was thrown from my car as it rolled. The doors were completely ripped off the car. I doubt I will ever know the truth about my accident.

When a cop called my mother at 2 in the morning, she could hear the swooping sound of the blades from the helicopter as it landed on the highway to take me to the I.C.U at UMass memorial in Worcester, Massachusetts. Doctors said if it had been too windy to fly the copter I would have died because an ambulance would have taken too long to get me to the hospital. I needed care and urgently. That was what happened to me April 19th 2006.

Riding in the ambulance after my month-long coma, Mom, begins to describe my injuries from the bottom up: I shattered my foot, collapsed a lung, broke my jaw, and I smashed my head into the window on the left side as blood pooled on the right killing nerves on that right side of the brain. This is what left me with left side neglect. "You had a five percent chance of living," Mom said, tears filling her eyes. "And on a coma scale where fifteen is the best, you were a three. This meant there was little hope for you. If you did survive you were supposed to be a vegetable."

The truth is, one night the doctors didn't think I would make it through to the morning. They told my father to stay as he readied to return home as he had to wake at four in the morning for work. They told him there was a good chance I wouldn't make it through the night. So my dad along with my mother and in shock stayed.

The tubes connected to my body each had a different function. There were of course the IV's so that my body would receive the correct amount of fluids. I had a brain tube, which helped pump fluid out of my brain. I had a chest tube, which pumped fluid out of my collapsed lung. I had these annoying leads or censors to measure my heart rate if it should fall below the correct amount of beats; because I was in great physical condition they would go off constantly because I had such a low heart rate. The tube that entered my stomach, filled with brown liquid, was filled with liquid nutrition. This is how I ate for more than a month because I still had my jaw wired shut.

Tasks that people don't think about in everyday life I had to learn all over again. I was a seventeen year old new-born. I had to learn how to speak, when to take the correct breaths as I spoke, I had to learn how to do basic math again, I had to learn how to walk, use my left hand, practice memory techniques, and correct my double vision.

The best way I can describe what a TBI (traumatic brain injury) is I had obtained a brain injury, by impact. Which is different from an acquired brain injury. An acquired brain injury is obtained by the body having a stroke, tumor, or degenerative diseases. They are not necessarily caused by an external source. A traumatic brain injury is caused by an outside source.

Waking up from a coma feels like any other day, like opening your eyes after a sleep. I had no recollection of what happened to me that night. A month later I wake up in a hospital bed. As I woke, I opened my eyes thinking it was just another typical day. My brain instantly calculated getting out of bed, making breakfast, and doing it all as quick as possible so I could hit the gym before school. As I tried to lift myself, out of bed, I found myself impaired. I mean, I've woken in a trunk before after a drunken stupor of a night but this was totally different.

I remember things, though, when I was in my coma. Because it was a medically induced coma, when I was slowly taken off the morphine or "waking up," I saw people crying. I would see their faces without understanding, and I'd drift in and out of sleep waking on occasion to see faces of tears and I'd return to sleep. I remember my Legion baseball coach, Sid, coming to visit me. And my football coach Jon Dubzinski and many, many of my friends. My parents wanted everyone to see what can happen to someone when they are reckless. Which I'm actually glad they did because hopefully it help guide people's decisions in the future. But what's funny about the whole thing is that it just feels like a dream. After seeing pictures and hearing stories about my coma, I have now developed more memories. When I see pictures, I think *Oh yeah, I remember that.* I believe that these pictures have actually brought back images that had been stored in my memory. That after seeing these pictures and refreshing my memory I do actually remember these things. I know Natasha would hold my hand, I would squeeze it. I don't remember if I heard her, if I smelled her or was even aware of her. But I know I squeezed her hand.

When I started waking I began to recognize all my friends and loved ones. Many were crying, but some were laughing. I thought *This is kind of an odd situation to be laughing in. Everyone else is crying.* As it turns out, my dad was cracking jokes to lighten the mood. Hun-dreds of my friends flooded the waiting room.

Many brought posters with pictures of me to reminisce the good times they had with "Zachy Chan" (my nickname in high school). My parents left the doors open so all my friends could see what could happen when someone acts carelessly. One minute you are on the top of the world and the next you are lying on a pile of leaves with blood oozing out of your head.

They couldn't believe this could happen to the nice kid who everyone loved. The happiest, most carefree kid one could meet now lies in a hospital bed with a five percent chance of living, connected to more tubes than one could believe barely keeping him alive.

As I was transferred to the rehab center by ambulance, most of my friends enjoyed life by the pool on a hot summer day. Not me. My summer would be filled with speech therapy and practicing how to walk. I lay in the ambulance as it took me from the I.C.U. at UMass Memorial in Worcestor to Spaulding rehab in Boston.

CHAPTER 2

REHABILITATION

N ow I was off to Boston. Soon I would be awakened to how cruel the world could be. Soon I would be taken by the hand, as if I was an infant, and have to learn to do everything over again. When I say everything that is exactly what I mean. I had to learn how to walk again, talk the correct way (when to take breaths at the correct time between words and phrases), how to use my left hand (which I still have a tough time directing), practice memory techniques/ strategies, learn math again and my balance and coordination were all screwed up due to the damage I had inflicted to my cerebellum.

The ambulance took me to Spaulding rehab in Boston. They wheeled me into the rehab center on a stretcher. Here I would do a stint of inpatient rehab. I assumed inpatient rehab meant I had to stay overnight. I had an optimistic outlook. I thought I would be in and out, get a few treatments as the night went on, and be perfectly normal. When I heard the doctors had me booked to stay for the entire summer, I buried my head into my sleeve as it lay on the table; while I sat in my wheelchair.

When I arrived they took down my weight. They weighed me on my bed because I could not get up; I couldn't even sit up on my own. The scale read a measly 121. I weighed around 150 before my accident. The nurses were afraid to give me too much food (liquid nutrition) in my coma, so I did not put on weight. Most of the weight I'd lost was in muscle I'd worked so hard over the years to develop. When I first came into the ICU the nurses felt my abs and they thought I had an abdominal injury because my abs were so hard. But now I no longer had hard abs, instead I had almost a pot belly. I actually thought that I was fat at my insignificant 121 pounds.

After a couple of days, I had regained sufficient strength to start my rehab. I started in a wheelchair. I hope to never sit in one of those again after being confined to one for a couple of weeks. They taught me how to transfer myself from the wheelchair to the bed, how to propel myself forward, and to make sure that my left hand, still weakened and almost useless, did not fall down into the spokes of the wheel. Becoming mobile again was great, but I wanted to be able to run, not wheel myself around in a wheelchair. For the most part my mom pushed me long distances. She stayed with me every night and every day and helped nursed me back to health.

After being a couple weeks it was time to get my jaw unwired. The speech pathologist had me opening my jaw as wide as I could while it was still wired to strengthen. Now instead of building muscle to hit home runs, I had to strengthen my jaw to chew food. I wondered what it would be like to again feel food in my mouth, to chew and swallow. I fantasized about all the flavors; chocolate, vanilla, strawberry. I would finally be able to taste food again! The nurses would tease me because they knew, even though I lay in a bed unable to move, I wouldn't let it hold me back from having a couple laughs. They often asked me what flavor liquid nutrition I wanted in my feeding tube on this day. I'd think really? I can't taste it, it's going directly into my stomach so I don't think it matters much.

When I went to get my jaw unwired, things went a little differently than I had anticipated. I thought there would be a long medical procedure to unwire them, maybe anesthesia, who knew. I anticipated the release of my mouth, but dreaded the steps to get me there. Nope! My mom wheeled me down a few floors to the room where it would take place. The doctor locked my wheels so I couldn't roll away and he busted out a hand tool similar to a screwdriver. He began twisting away on the inside of my mouth. I could feel the repetitive tug on my mouth. One by one he released metal pieces in my mouth into a metal tray. A few minutes into it he clapped his hands together and said, "You're all set." "Well that was an experience," I thought. After the ordeal, I continually rubbed my jaw and opened it as wide as I could, but the first thing I did was go down a couple floors to the food court and get something to eat. I still had limitations to what I could eat. I couldn't have the steak that I wanted, so I got chocolate pudding. It was the best tasting pudding I have ever had.

When I attempted to walk with a walker or on a treadmill, my knee would always bend backwards and would hurt, a lot. It was more of a quick snap than a bend. A man came in to make a half cast molded to my foot all the way up to my knee. It gave my left knee support and would stop my knee from hyper-extending when I stood. The man asked if I wanted a picture or a decal on the back. I could actually communicate with words now instead of nodding or pointing at things. I told him that I wanted a Red Sox decal, but they did not have any Red Sox decals. The only decals they had for sports teams were the Patriots; I decided to suck it up and go with the Patriots decal. Don't get me wrong I love the Pats, but I'm a baseball guy.

When I first started to learn how to walk again, my therapist would crouch next to me as I grasped a cane in my right hand. In her crouch, she would pick up my leg and help it swing. She would give me commands on what she wanted me to do. She would say, "Heel, toe, knee, swing." Then repeat the process. She would tell me to repeat the commands in my head or say them out loud, even. I would go to an hour of physical therapy a day, an hour of occupational therapy a day and an hour of speech therapy a day. But I would practice walking with my mom for hours.

It was hard for me to learn how to walk because my leg did not know the correct movements, but also because if my concentration ran off to something else I would lose my balance and fall (which with a brain injury, I often lost my concentration). Walking down the hall was difficult. When I had to make a turn, I had to slow down, almost to a complete stop. One time I was turning the corner in the main hallway to go into the cafeteria, I moved too fast, tripped over my own foot and fell right into a motorized wheelchair. My mother ran to my side and helped me up. I got up as fast as I could, looked to make sure nobody saw, and continued on my journey to get something to drink.

To get my brain back in control of my left arm and hand the doctors would only let me use my left hand. Though I was right-handed naturally, from writing to balance to throwing a baseball, I now had to use my left hand for everything. Little things, things you don't even think about. I had to use my left hand to brush my teeth and pick up my cup to drink from. They joked, for the recovery, it would be best if they tied my right hand behind my back. They didn't of course, but it would admittedly have made things easier.

One means of therapy used to strengthen my left hand was therapists putting little tiny Christmas bulbs in a hard, thick putty. They would make me pick out each of the little tiny bulbs. I used to be able to bench press over 200 lbs. Now, picking up tiny light bulbs was my exercise. This was a tedious task, and half-way through the exercise my arm would be on fire. It was so hard for me to find the concentration to focus on picking out every last bulb, and I had very little control of my hand. Not to mention my arm hurt tremendous amounts during this exercise. I was told it was the nerves reestablishing a connection. As I focused on picking out every bulb, tiny beads of sweat would stream down my face. I cannot explain to you, in words, how frustrating it is to relearn these tasks. To one day make progress and the next day you're back where you initial started.

I have always been a moma's boy since I can remember. It's kind of embarrassing. My mom used to do everything for me, and actually still does a lot for me as funny as that may sound. But, now I am an even bigger moma's boy. She stayed with me through everything. She quit her job because her first born baby boy was in the hospital. She stayed with me every night that I was in ICU and now she was going to be by my side for the whole time I would remain in inpatient rehab. She slept on the most uncomfortable of things, she slept on what looked like metal and iron twisted together to make a pull-out sleeping surface. I owe my life to my mom. She helped me so much and made sure I pushed myself even harder than I would have pushed myself. My mom would say things like, "If you ever want to get on that field again we are going to have to work extremely hard." She would always throw a "we" in there, this way I never felt alone.

She took me on walks so I could practice once I had my four prong cane. But over time she encouraged me to walk without it, "Walk without it, the last day of rehab you're walking out of here without it." This was not permitted because of my balance. To describe what it was like to walk without balance, it was like constantly walking on a balance beam even though the ground upon which I walked might have been a shopping mall parking lot. Everything seemed only a few inches wide. On frequent walks I would do what felt to me like sprints, back and forth. These were not the conventional sprints that you are probably thinking of. But they felt like sprints to me because I had no endurance from being bedridden for an entire month. To you, all I did was walk back and forth. To me, these were 5am practice suicide sprints.

Near where I would walk was a window with a view out into the back bay of Boston. By the back bay of Boston were two baseball fields. I used to take breaks from walking and just gaze upon the fields. I pledged to myself that one day I would be able to walk out onto that field again and be the player that I used to be.

Everyday, I would lie in my hospital bed and listen to my IPod, unable to move and unable to go anywhere. Stuck in a netted bed, I would go through my playlist to pass the time, but there was one song in particular I would listen to over and over, every day. The song was *Days Go By* by Keith Urban. The chorus of this song filled me with hope and inspiration, that one day I would finally escape rehab and be able to walk again, and hopefully be a normal person again. I would hear "and days go by . . ." and it would make me realize that though it didn't feel like it, I actually was making progress.

The bed they allowed me was a bed surrounded by a net. Every time I watched T.V., I was forced to watch through a net. Whenever I had to pee late at night I would go in a bottle instead of calling a nurse to help me to the bathroom. The bottle did spill on occasion. I had no coordination to hold the bottle from shaking. They kept me in this prison-like bed because people with brain injuries tend to think they are able to do things when they really can't, like walk. This bed kept me secure, for the most part.

One evening, trapped like a prisoner in my own bed, I had to pee really, really bad. As I peered through the net I saw how close the sink was to the bed. I thought, "I can walk pretty well now. If I can hold myself up for a second I could lean toward the counter of the sink, I could support my weight and grab the handles and railings around the room to make it to the bathroom."

When my mom left to get food in the cafeteria in one of the lower floors, she zipped the bed shut, but there was just enough room for me to fit my hand through. I stuck my hand through the opening, gripped one of the zippers from the outside and started to unzip the bed. Each side of the oval-shaped hole had to be unzipped. It seemed to take forever, but I was motivated by the thought that I would, for the first time, walk myself to the bathroom. Finally, it was unzipped, the hole opened.

I placed myself on the side of the bed, feet dangling, they hovered over the floor. "You can do this, Zach. You can do this, Zach" I repeated to myself. I carefully went over the plan once more. "All I need to do is get to the sink and the rest is cake." I planted both feet on the floor, raised my butt off the bed. I was lying on the ground in a matter of seconds. I don't know what happened, but I was on the floor. My feeding tube fell out of my stomach on the way to the floor and was spilling liquid nutrition everywhere.

My mom finally returned. I was sprawled on the floor laughing hysterically as large amounts of liquid nutrition spilled all over my body, hair and face. My mom began to yell at me. She said something like *Zach! What are you doing!* She picked me up and threw me into bed like I was a sack of rice. After the ordeal was over I said to her, "Sorry, I thought if I . . . ." and I stopped. I could see on her face how mad she was; it wasn't as funny as I thought. In fact, I realized, I could have caused a major setback in my rehab.

Occasionally on a weekend I would receive a pass to go home. I was so excited to see all my friends, and every weekend I went home it was an event. Everyone that I knew would come to my house, or wherever I would end up, to see me. Not just my friends; people that I saw passing in the halls in high school came to see me. I was friendly with everyone that I came in contact with. I believe you should be kind to others because you'll never know when you'll need them to do something for you, or just be there for support. I needed friends now and they were not shy about showing their support.

On those weekends, I would get out of the car, receive help from my father or mother as I got into my wheelchair. As I got out of the car a huge roar would erupt. They would make signs and put them up all over. Signs that read 'Welcome home Zach.' These signs and these moments of love meant so much to me, I can't quite express it. It is one reason I kept pushing on.

One of the symptoms of the brain injury was I'd developed double vision because one of my left eye muscles was not strong enough to keep my eye straight, so it floated up. I would see two of everything. Two doctors, two moms, two girlfriends, which I guess wasn't too bad. I needed to find a temporary solution for this problem. I tried everything. An eye patch, glasses with one of the lens' fogged up, glasses with prisms built in, but when I took them off I saw two of everything. I required eye surgery for a permanent fix, which I would not get until I was home for good.

My girlfriend, Natasha, wrote a book for me as I lay in my coma. Every night she wrote a journal entry for me about things she was feeling; if I had a good day or a bad day, how much she missed me, how if I ever did anything like this again she would kill me. Topics like that filled the book. I started to read it when I was in inpatient rehab. But because my double vision was so bad, I found out later it said something completely different than what I had thought. I realized that when I read the words that I was actually inserting what I thought she would have written rather than what was actually written. For example, I thought the book would be filled with how much she missed me, the book did have this, mostly she wrote about things relating to how good or bad my brain was functioning based on the reading from the machines. I thought the book was all about everything she missed doing with me, etc. Weird I know, but you try reading with double vision and severe brain damage.

It was very difficult to read, well it's really difficult to do anything when you see two of everything. You see two images, which look the exact same. You never know which one to look at. I would feel bad when people would talk to me because I would look away from them and it must have appeared that I didn't care about what they were saying. I saw one image that was unclear and cloudy, and I saw another image that was unclear and cloudy. In time one would become more pronounced and I would realize the one on the right was the real object, the one I needed to focus on.

A nurse helper (student) from North Eastern University came to follow me around all day to see what my life in rehab was like. In other words, she wanted to study who Zach was after his brain injury. Because she was a student there, I told her how I was getting scouted by North Eastern University for baseball. I said I wished I could play at that level again and play for NE. She simple responded "Why not?" That simple statement will stick with me forever. Whenever someone tells me I **can't** do something I think back to what she said. She gave me more motivation; she helped me believe that my goal wasn't just a dream, that it was actually attainable.

I can't explain what it feels like to spend hours and days and weeks of your life to earn something and because of one night, every moment of those hours is worthless. All your hard work down the drain "for nothing", I thought to myself. I worked so hard for baseball, to be a great athlete, and once I was on the path leading to my dream, I had to get involved with alcohol and ruin my life. I worked so hard, looking back on it, I didn't have a childhood. I was always at the field hitting three buckets of balls with my dad or shagging fly balls. I didn't mind because this is what I enjoyed doing. I would rather be on the ballfield than play video games or whatever a normal kid does.

Most people, the overwhelming majority of all of humanity, have no idea what it was like to lie in a wheelchair unable to move or talk. Everyone comes to visit because they figure you're lonely (which I was) and they try to cheer you up. But how much can they cheer you up? You're in constant pain for reasons you cannot explain. Your back starts to ache and you have no idea why. Everyone who visits comes bearing gifts. They stay for a half an hour and crack jokes to get a smile out of you.

So, I play along with it and laugh. But, the funny thing was I had nothing to laugh about. Yeah, I was alive, but did I really want to live this life where my only means of transportation is a chair with wheels? So all my friends would ask, "Zach, is something wrong?" and I would think to myself "I'm great, never been better, I can't walk, can't talk, can't think fast enough to process your statements, can't eat and can't stay awake for the life of me." So I smiled and nodded and played it off like I was still the same old Zach who was full of joy and always happy.

When I say that I had to relearn everything, this includes even those things we do subconsciously. Like controlling bodily functions pertaining to urine and feces. To ensure that I didn't have an "accident" at night I was forced to sleep with a diaper. Every morning, the night nurses would come in and check on me. They would roll me over to see if I had wet myself. They would roll me over, back and forth, to check both sides. Just like a mother would do to a newborn.

I had no idea how to tie my shoes! I came home one weekend and struggled to tie my shoes. I could not figure it out and my motor skills were all messed up. Just trying to hold "the bunny ears" of the shoestrings was a task. Every time I tried the stupid bunny ears, or the stupid loop swoop and pull thing, they would fall. Or it felt like they would just explode in my hands into lone laces again. I got so frustrated. I would just look up at God and ask, "Why, what have I done so wrong?" Everyone would say, "Oh Zach, it's not the end of the world." But they weren't in my shoes, unable to tie them. I just wanted to be normal again. The little things are worse for someone brain injured; you feel messed up because of your brain injuries. I'm still more mad at the tiny things than things of importance. Even after all this time I have to learn self-control. I've improved, but the small things still drive me mad.

I would have never of figured out how to tie my shoes if it weren't for Natasha. When home sitting on my couch, I tried to tie my shoes again, letting out angry sighs in front of everyone. I was miserable and I knew everyone could see it. After all, what kind of baseball player can't tie his own shoes within seconds? Natasha reached down and tied my shoes for me. I was like, "How did you do that?" She broke down the steps for me, even took my hands and helped me move my hands/fingers accordingly. I was so proud of myself I was absolutely pumped!

As I left rehab, I exceeded everyone's expectations. The rehab center dubbed me Miracle Kid. Instead of staying the whole summer I was out in two months. I could walk on my own, but I preferred a cane because my balance wasn't that great and I would fall when my concentration wandered. I had decent use of my left hand and arm, but it wasn't great. It moved slower than my right hand and it was much harder to control. I had come far for everyone else's standards, but not mine. I still had much further to go far more than I realized, to accomplish my goal of being able to play baseball again.

CHAPTER 3

ADAPTATION

The summer following my accident was terrible. My life was now consumed by rehab, make-up work so that I would graduate on time, and my brother's baseball games (I hated going to my brother's games). Instead of sipping on drinks by the pool, working or playing baseball, my life now consisted of practicing walking and practicing the correct way to solve an algorithm.

My little league coach, Jeff Dedian, hosted a fundraiser on July 4th, 2006 at the Leominster Babe Ruth Field. There were hundreds of people there and they all came to see and support me. It was incredible how many people had come out in my honor. I was only out of rehab for about one week. For recreation we had a couple of pickup games of baseball, softball and even a home run derby. It was a great day of events enjoyed by everyone. Over $22,000 was raised for rehab that I had to continue at Burbank Hospital in Fitchburg and Ramsey Rehab Leominster. The money also went towards paying remaining medical bills.

On the days I didn't get tutored I was in outpatient rehab for several hours. I had speech therapy to learn cognitive skills and how to pronounce words again. I had occupational therapy to help me understand how to do things with my disability. All this followed by physical therapy to work on balance, walking, and things of that nature. Every single day I would have at least one of the three.

The upside to this round of rehab was living at home and going to a hospital rather than living in a hospital. Doing rehab here gave me more freedom than when I was at Spaulding. I was starting to walk on my own without assistance pretty well. To test my progress, my physical therapist strapped a belt around my waist and told me to walk on the grass down a hill. He trailed me closely with a hand between my back and the belt. Whenever I would start to waiver or lose my balance in the slightest he would give a quick tug of the belt to steady and balance me.

Before I could consider driving I had to work on reflexes to react for the unpredictability of the road. My occupational therapist first gave me a test to examine my road rule knowledge for acquiring a driving license. I passed with flying colors. To test my reaction time, she held a green ball and a red ball. She told me to stomp on her foot when the light turned red. She held up the green ball, wiggling it in my face then she would move the red ball into view. I would move my foot over hers and press slightly. I passed this test as well.

It made me sad to go to my Brother Mike's baseball games. In fact, I hated the routine of going. But I went anyway to cheer for my little bro. He was having a great season and he was having so much fun on and off the field. I envied him. I hated going to his baseball games. I hated going to the game watching my brother happy doing something that made me that happy. Baseball was my life. I breathed, daily, the game of baseball. Sitting in the bleachers that summer I would think, "This is so unfair. Why does he get to have so much fun and be happy?" Don't get me wrong, I was happy for my brother. I was mad that he could have all this fun and I was left out. I would never confront him about it, but I was always envious watching him run in the outfield.

Although I walked with a cane and began to learn how to walk without it, coaches still asked me about the flaws in players' swings. Or they would ask me to talk to the team and tell them about my experiences playing. While I was honored to provide guidance and motivation, these experiences almost brought me to tears. I relived over and over all the good times with my teammates and playing baseball all summer. I used to worry I may never have this much fun or get to have the type of camaraderie I got when on a baseball diamond ever again.

I had doctors tell me that there was no medical explanation to why I was alive, never mind walking, talking, or functioning for that matter. Doctors couldn't believe the strides I had made in such a short time span. Looking back on it, I believe the only way I made such great gains was due to the fact I wasn't willing to let the accident ruin my life.

I looked at it this way; my life could suck now, while I put in all this hard work, or it could suck the rest of my life and I could be confined to a wheelchair unable to work, go to school, be with my friends, etc. Hard work was the only real option. That and the fact God had his hands on me.

Oh, I almost forgot there was a minor problem when I was learning how to walk. My foot was broken and I could not get surgery because that would require me being bedridden. The first six months after a brain injury is when you make the most progress, and they needed me to continue walking as often as I could even though my foot had bone chips in it. I could not afford to lose any opportunity for recovery time because of how bad the accident left me, and the small window for helping the body and brain bounce back. So, for the first three months I had to learn how to walk all over again, with a broken foot.

Another requirement that summer was to make up classes I'd missed in order to progress from my junior to senior year. My least favorite subject, math, became my most difficult after the accident. Before the accident it was already my most difficult. Because of my brain injury, I had damaged the right side of my brain so badly and the right side of the brain deals with cognition. I lost all my math skills. Mr. Rooney, a family friend and math teacher at Leominster High School, requested he be my tutor. I was, technically, in my first grade of math. I was essentially learning how to do basic math problems from the ground up and yet trying to achieve, within the summer, junior level math.

The summer stretched on and daily I was reminded I would have to learn how to adapt to everyday life. My mom, my physical therapist, everyone, talked about the changes that would have to be made for me to assimilate to everyday life. But mentally, in my soul, I went into the summer thinking I was normal. Ignorance is bliss. I didn't think I was as bad as I actually was. I believe this helped because I never thought there was anything I couldn't do, in time. I thought I was normal and held myself to the standards of every other normal person around me. Yes, this caused me a lot of stress, but it helped me push myself, it helped me not be afraid to fail.

By the end of summer, I walked without a cane and talked a lot better. My speech, still slurred, sounded much better. I didn't need to take as many break in between words to catch my breath as I spoke. I struggled with my math skills, and still do for that matter, but I was weak in math before brain damage.

People close to me were very supportive. Natasha, Mike, my parents were all there for me. This included all of my friends, but over time I would find out who my true friends were. Many people wanted to show their support the moment it happened to me. But as time went on, those who stayed by my side became friends for life. The whole city of Leominster was supportive of me and the struggles I faced in recovery. Stories about my recovery flooded the newspaper. Everywhere I went, people knew who I was and I would always hear, "You're a miracle" or "Such an inspiration."

Finally, it was football season. This was the year, my senior year, I was slated to be captain of the varsity football team. I'd waited for this moment my entire football career. And as it turned out, I was the captain. But I had to watch my senior season from the sidelines. I sat week after week knowing that I was better than some of the kids out there. I'd see a ridiculous play or a dumb move and think, "Damn, if I were playing that would have never happened." My future was in baseball, even before the accident, so no matter what had happened in my life, there was no doubt my senior year of football would be the last I'd play in a team setting for the rest of my life. What I could not have known was that my junior year, last year was in reality the last I'd ever play football in a team setting. It was hard knowing the last time I could play football, I couldn't all because of some stupid mistake. Nonetheless, as team captain, I was there every practice/ game to support my team.

Sometimes I would attempt to lead the team around the field for the opening lap. More often than not I wasn't able to make it around the field. I would move off to the sideline and motion for the team to move ahead. My left leg would shake wildly; I would stop it by putting pressure through my leg to my heel and straighten my leg. I would do calisthenics with the team to practice my running. I like to think that I earned a lot of respect from my teammates, and in my pushing myself they would push themselves in return; that was the most important thing to me-and my biggest contribution that season.

I spent my entire summer sending out emails to division one and division two schools telling them what had happened to me. Most schools interested in me before my accident had no interest now. However, my reputation preceded me. I received several letters from college coaches.

I even received a letter from the UMass Lowell coach, Ken Harring, handwritten telling me he wanted me no matter what. It was kind of a small school (I thought I'd like a bigger school), I didn't like the location of the school, and it just wasn't a good fit for me. I honestly didn't even care about what I studied; all I cared about was playing baseball. I sent a letter to the UMass Amherst coach, Coach Stone. We emailed back and forth during the school year, and he was really supportive. I began to look at this school more closely. I set up a meeting with Coach Stone and I even ended up going on an un-official visit and stayed with one of the players. I stayed in contact with coach stone because I had my eyes set on playing division 1 baseball. We emailed back and forth throughout the year.

So, before the accident, I had all these friends, or so I thought. I certainly was wanted at parties and felt very popular. One of my good friends, Jon Rodriguez, or Jrod, used to say "a friend is nothing but a dollar in your pocket." I never knew what he meant until the accident happened. I had so many friends and they all came to see me when I was hospitalized and they'd come out to public fundraisers, but then I went back trying to live normal and they realized that I was different. When I really needed friends they were nowhere to be found. They supported me when it was convenient, and when they'd be seen as public fundraising supporters, but I was different now. I might embarrass them if we were out in public. That's when I discovered who my TRUE friends were.

I had a group of friends that stuck by my side through it all. They always invited me to do stuff and hangout, even if I did make a semi-rude comment about someone or something. See, the problem was that I had to learn to be a polite and not impulsive. It wasn't until I got to college that I was able to see I was being inappropriate. I later developed a *don't speak until spoken to* attitude to control myself. I ended up alienating myself, but it was the only way to teach myself to relax. In college, people didn't know me or know that I had a brain injury. Obviously, they wouldn't understand or want to hear random outbursts of inappropriate behavior.

In high school, my friends who saw me change thought because I was strange, I would always be strange. Very few gave me a chance to learn and improve. Except my true friends; they all knew I would say or do things a little out of the ordinary. They took pride in being my friend. They knew I'd heal, become normal again. They would laugh at my obscene joke or joke around with me about my disability. We used to play this game Apples to Apples and any time someone would say car accident or coma, I became the brunt of their joke. I embraced this; it made me feel like I was like every other kid out there.

I always thought to myself thank God for Natasha. She was the one holding me together. Without her I would have been lost and lonely. She always (at the beginning of my senior year) brought me things to show she cared. She always wanted to be with me no matter what happened. She helped me walk by making sure my path was clear and helped me do things that I couldn't, such as if my left arm was not strong enough to grab or hold on to something, she would help. She was a great girl.

When I finally had surgery on my foot right before my senior year began, Natasha came over and brought me ice cream and stayed with me for the night. But my surgery was extremely painful; Doctors had to take the bone chips out of my foot and then they shaved down the bone of my foot. The doctors said, "Oh yah, you will definitely be able to walk immediately after you get out of surgery." So I begin to think to myself, "This isn't going to be that bad. I mean, I learned how to walk for three months with a broken foot. How bad could it be?"

I stepped down from the hospital bed after I woke from the anesthesia and screamed in agonizing pain. I yelled, "They lied" and hollered stuff like, "You are going to be able to walk my ass!" I was absolutely furious at the doctors for lying. I honestly couldn't put any pressure on my foot. This meant I was going to have to use a wheelchair, again, to get out of this building. I was so angry! I hated wheelchairs!

After being confined to a chair as your only means of transportation for a month or so, I cannot describe to you what it feels like to finally be able to walk again and able to move around on your own, then have it taken away. I was right back where I started in rehab. I thought to myself, "You got to be kidding me . . . . God this isn't fair . . . why me!?"

I truly believe that I will never feel such an intense pain ever again. This wasn't simple pain, this was something else, this was pain on steroids. I couldn't move. I just sat on the couch trying not to drink too much water because otherwise I'd have to go to the bathroom and that was a process in itself. Once again, thanks to this foot surgery, I needed three people to help carry me and help keep pressure off of my foot. I would sit on the toilet to take a piss. That wasn't the worse part. I couldn't move that well, I was so uncoordinated. So, to position myself on the seat, it seemed to take forever. I had to keep my healthy foot on the ground and pivot around it. Since my right foot, the one I usually favored as I was right-handed, was the one all bandaged and cut from the surgery, not to mention the bone in that foot was shaven down, any pressure on that foot was excruciating. I couldn't move my left foot well enough to pivot with the foot that didn't hurt. I had to pivot on the foot just operated on. I cannot describe to you in words how badly it hurt.

I was in so much pain. And I yelled when I put my weight on my foot like a little bitch. I screamed so loud I was embarrassed because many of my friends were visiting and Natasha was there. Once I finally got back from the bathroom and sat down, I just looked up to God and prayed, "God, there must be a reason why . . . I know you are not putting me through this for no reason, what is it?"

Not only did the doctors leave me in excruciating pain they also left a stitch in my foot! Every time I would put on a sock, shoe, or accidently rub up against something it would hurt. It was very difficult for me to sleep because my foot and my stitch rubbed against the lightest of sheets and I would be in immense pain. In time, whatever caused the immense pain, eventually began to heal. The pain subsided. It worked its way through the skin and discharged itself from my body.

After I finally learned how to walk without a cane near the end of summer, I noticed I had developed what I considered a nervous habit. My left hand, instead of hanging by my side, would flex and keep my arm at a seventy-five degree angle. I wasn't even trying to flex, but you could see the muscles in my forearm flexing. This was called muscle tone; because the nerves in my brain that controlled my arm were damaged, my arm was in a constant state of partially flexing. If I concentrated, I could keep it by my side or even swing it in sync with my right arm, but the minute I lost focus it would go into that seventy five degree angle position.

After the injury, I flirted with almost every girl I saw. Because of my reputation of being a 'ladies man' before the accident, people just thought this part of my personality hadn't changed. They assumed that I personally made the choice to flirt with every girl. But the reality was more like my brain was confused and didn't know the correct way to show affection. Even the early years following my accident, when I was in college, girls were afraid to get close to me. They all assumed I wanted sex and I was going out of my way to flirt with them. Reality was, I just wanted to be friends. But because of my injury I would want some form of contact (hug, kiss on the cheek, etc.), and I felt this was the proper way to show affection; to show care and concern.

Not surprising, Natasha was one who didn't understand what compelled me to flirt or be overly affectionate. She did not get why I felt like I had to flirt with every girl I passed or met in high school. Later, after I broke-up with her and even later asked for her back, she listed this as a problem. Even though I'd ceased to compulsively flirt, she still held it against me because of my behavior when my brain was all confused. It must have sucked to be her, retrospect, being out with me and yet me flirting with other girls right in front of her. I also had trouble expressing my personality. It is very difficult for me to describe what it is like to not be able to control your actions. It was almost like someone had complete control of me, like in a video game; I knew what I did often was inappropriate, but I couldn't stop myself.

Oftentimes I was mean to people when I felt I was kidding around. They would think that I really hated them when in fact I was just trying to crack jokes at their expense in what I thought was a completely friendly way. In college I discovered why girls thought I was a "creep." Over time, I avoided women in an attempt to bring some normality to my life. This too, left me alone and alienated in college.

My schedule for my senior year in high school consisted of half days every day so I could continue my out-patient rehab at Ramsey. Even though I was doing half days, I was extremely exhausted. I would get to rehab and prefer to sleep rather than practice my balance. I would often do my rehab in the pool. I loved being in the small rehab pool because I felt normal. The feeling of weightlessness was incredible. I couldn't hop on my left foot on land, but I could in the water. It was one of the few times I felt free from this injury, able to do everything I'd always done.

Sometimes I would do rehab with the elderly, many of them stroke victims. We had the same symptoms, same lasting effects, with one major difference. I would have an easier time recovering because of my youth. If I had gotten in this accident at sixty or seventy, I might never have recovered.

One day in class my name was called on the school intercom. "Zach Gauvin, please report to Coach Dubziski's office." Bewildered, I began to make my way down to his office. Coach Dubziski was my football coach. Why would my coach want to see me? A stranger waited with a camera, pen and notepad as I entered the office.

"Zach, this man would like to run a piece on you in a magazine."

The name of the magazine was CMass Sports Insider. He took pictures of me standing tall, looking off into the distance holding a football. One of these photos landed on the cover of the magazine. He interviewed me about life before and after the accident. He asked questions about why I worked so hard to get back. And at the end of the article my answer appeared.

"I want to go division one. Because I know I can. And I'm gonna."

My brain was still swollen. I was not given a timetable as to when the swelling would subside completely, but I had to take and pass the SATs to go to college. Many of the subjects and questions of the test I'd forgotten, but the worst aspect was that because my brain worked so hard during the test, and so soon after my accident, my brain felt like it had swollen even more. It felt like that my brain actually grew in size and gave me a severe headache. I don't know if you know what it's like to attempt to concentrate when your eyeballs feel like they are being pushed out of your skull, but this is how I felt.

I did the best I could on the exam under the circumstances, but as you can imagine, my scores weren't very good. I went home after the test, went to bed and threw up until I was drained. I tried to forget about the pain in my head, but it was impossible. Light was my enemy that day causing excruciating pain. I attempted to make my room as dark as I could, but nothing would help. I ended up getting an 1130 on all three of the SAT tests combined, a very poor score.

My mother always tried to help me with hand-eye coordination. One time I was in the kitchen making a sandwich. My mother came up behind and started talking about how I needed to use my left hand more.

"The only way for you to get it back is to use it," she said, often. I would answer back, "I know! I'm doing everything I can mom!"

My mom hit my shoulder and said, "Cmon!" She held her hand up, like a target. I answered back, "What?" I was confused with what she wanted out of me.

"Hit my hand!" she said.

"Mom, I'm not going to punch you."

"Just do it!"

After several minutes of arguing, I gave up and threw a punch toward her hand. I made contact, but not with her hand. I punched my mother flat in the nose.

Horrified, I asked, "Are you okay?"

She laughed with tears coming to her eyes. "Yes, I'm fine. You were so close."

Thanksgiving Day game was here. Leominster v.s. Fitchburg, one of the oldest rivalries in the nation, and I couldn't play. I itched to get out there as I sat on the sidelines watching my team kill Fitchburg. I suited up for the game because my friend Dean, the quarterback, and I planned that I would run out for a play. It was hard because I had an excellent game the year before, making one of the most athletic plays I had ever made in a football game. I knocked down a pass over the middle of the field. But this wasn't last year, this was this year. I was different now.

As the game-clock counted down, I highly anticipated my chance to run out on the field. Then coach called my name. He told me to get out to wide receiver. The crowd erupted as I ran onto the field. As I got in my stance, I watched everyone from the stands get as close to the field as possible in case anyone from Fitchburg tried to mess with me. I ran in and I'm pretty sure I lined-up offside because I couldn't stop my body momentum. I heard "Hut!" and as fast as it started, the play was over. I ran back to the sidelines as everyone cheered for me. I couldn't stop my left leg from shaking. I was so excited with what had just happened. Natasha, watched from the stands and cheered with excitement. This was also one of the goals my mom and I set during rehab. We wanted for me to run on the field in the Thanksgiving game. I did it. Later I found out that I had made headlines all over, in the Sentinel and Enterprise, Boston Globe and even NFL.com.

With all the emotion being displayed by fans, teammates, and my coach, I lost how amazing this moment was. It felt awesome to be on the field with my teammates again. I tried to treat it like it wasn't a big deal. After all, this was one of my goals, but it was not my number one goal. Until I accomplished the goal of baseball I could not be satisfied.

Just one goal down many more to go.

I felt it was my fault that I couldn't play. I felt my stupid mistake had let everyone down. We made it to the super bowl (championship between western and central Mass.), but we lost. Even though we lost 42-0, I felt we could have won if I was able to play. I know what you're saying. "Wow, 42-0 . . . you guys got killed." But the funny thing is that we played the same team in the super bowl a year before, where I was the starting cornerback and occasionally wide-receiver, and we only lost by one point. I blamed myself and felt like I was the missing component.

I only applied to one college, the University of Massachusetts at Amherst. I was recruited and that was my biggest factor in my decision. I was listed as a recruited walk-on. Despite my SAT's being a low 1130, I had no problem getting in. I was a recruit, my grades were good and I was unique. I wrote my college essay about what I had experienced waking up from my coma. I applied early action and even with the option to decline their offer, I didn't apply anywhere else.

New Year of 2007 came, and I ended up being the number one sports story for the year 2006 for my hometown newspaper. The readers had the vote and they voted for my story. The title: "Gauvin's Miraculous Recovery." The article was about what I went through, where I wanted to go, and things I had already accomplished. It was a nicely written piece, but it made me realize and think about how far I had to go.

Soon after the article, I got this great idea that I wanted to be on Youtube. Why, I do not know. I thought it would be fun to take advantage of myself in the name of humor. After the accident I couldn't really feel pain, so I thought nothing could hurt me and I wanted to show my confidence to the world. I told my friends to line me up as a firing squad would line up a prisoner and in the blistering cold shoot me in my back with an air soft gun as many times until I moved away. I was shirtless. My friend recorded this on a camera. I think we got to twelve shots before I moved out of the way. My back blistered and welted horribly. We went back to my friend Thomas' house and did more things to inflict pain to myself. We dropped a basketball on my testicles. We did everything we could think of so that I could show the world my indestructible resolve.

We then put the video on Youtube, and literally everyone in the school saw it.

The next day at school, everyone who worked on the video with me was called down to the office. They then called me into a separate room with the school psychologist. To summarize the two meetings; the principal told my friends they were terrible friends for doing that to me and the psychologist thought they had taken advantage of me. They said the same thing I did, and the truth, that it was all my idea. We were forced to pull the Youtube video or else we couldn't walk during graduation. All in all, I think I would do it again. We were just a bunch of dumb kids trying to have fun.

The whole winter I went to Sid's cages a couple times a week to train to get back on the baseball field. We would hit for an hour straight. I always thought that I was going to be able to play again because of the way Sid talked. He would get me all hyped and made me believe in myself that I could do it. I made pretty good contact for seeing two balls, just had to remember "it's the one on the right."

As baseball season opened, I was still named captain and would hit, field, and run with the team. Whatever they were doing I did the best of my ability. I would get stressed because my recovery was taking so long. I would get stressed because if I didn't heal in time I wouldn't be able to play baseball at the level I wanted. I got in to hit a couple times and I walked, got hit by a pitch, and one time I almost got a hit. The pitch came in and I roped it down the first baseline, but foul. When I say I roped it, I mean I hit an absolute laser, but of course it went foul and the next pitch I struck out. Though it was an eventual strike-out, it felt incredible to hit the ball. The crack of the bat, the vibration in my arms; all exhilarating. On my way back to the dugout, I kept saying to myself, "If I can make contact like that, I'm going to play."

Near the end of my senior year of high school Jon Hernandez, or Jhern, and I were being recognized by the state for football. He had won an All-State award for defensive back, and I had won an award for courage. Jon's award was to acknowledge his achievements on the field; my award was to acknowledge everything that I went through. My award was way cooler than Jon's. He got a piece of paper and I got a bust. It was the upper half of an old time football player, with the leather helmet, etc. I had won the Henry J. Smith courage award of 2006. It was a very prestigious award given to me by the Grid Iron Club of Greater Boston. It is probably one of the most prestigious awards I own. Out of a very populated Massachusetts, only four won this award that year. I stood on stage proudly; I hoisted my trophy.

On my senior prom night, Natasha had to carry my food and drinks. I was so embarrassed I could not carry my own food. The whole night Natasha and I danced with my good friend Jon Hernandez and his girlfriend, the love of his life Kaylin. We danced as everyone around us got into trouble for drinking.

Natasha and I didn't have sex after prom, which I thought was odd. I thought it was odd because we had had sex after our junior prom, so why not senior? I also thought this was strange because we were in love. This is kind of embarrassing to say, but also kind of funny. Right when I got out of rehab I was not strong enough to hold myself up to be on top. My arms would shake while I held myself over her, so the length of time for me on top was *very* limited. We had to switch often. But I think in time this actually helped me developed strength/ stamina in other activities.

Soon after came my graduation party. I split my party with a couple of kids and we had a good time. We rented out a dance hall and there was food and drinks. Natasha didn't come until the end of the party as she said she wanted to go to another high school prom. I began to wonder how things would work out between us. Our relationship had begun to deteriorate.

It was summer, which meant it was legion baseball season. I was excited to see all of my friends that had gone off to college the year before. Coach Rafuse told me that he wanted me on the team, but there wasn't enough roster space. He listed me as a coach instead, which meant I couldn't get on the field like I had during the high school season. He told all the players to respect me as their coach. I didn't mind because it freed up space for someone who could actually participate and help out the team. I went to every game and every practice that season as if I was on the team, even though I was a "coach." I enjoyed the thrill of coaching and also learned a lot from Sid, Jeff and some of the other coaches. But I still couldn't wrap my head around the fact that I was not out there, playing, making amazing catches, making the art of hitting look so easy. No, instead I watched as my teammates took to the field without me, day-in and day-out.

You know how baseball players wear cleats, but they wear sandals when they are not on the field so that they do not wear down their cleats? Well, I could not wear sandals because when I walked my left leg kicked out, and when I walked up stairs my brain did not tell my feet to scrunch my toes to grab on to the sandals. Sandals always fell off when I walked up stairs. Because I could not wear sandals I sought an alternative to my foot wear problem.

I wouldn't wear any shoes.

You know how hard and dangerous it is to drive without shoes or sandals? I kept one sandal in my car, called it 'my driving shoe' and I would slip it on so I could drive safely. After I parked I would take it off and leave it in my car and walk out shoeless. I constantly stepped on twigs, rocks, whatever was on the ground. My feet were super sensitive because my nerves were all messed up in my head, and I would sometimes feel terrible pain. I needed to find a better way.

My friend Gaetanno always wore boating shoes instead of sandals in the summer. He often wore them like sandals (without socks and with shorts). I thought to myself, "This is it, finally I can have some footwear that could easily slip on and off." I would go to the games wearing my brown boating shoes and everyone would question what I had on my feet. I just smiled and laughed. A chuckle beats the pain any day.

CHAPTER 4

ALL ON MY OWN

T oward the end of the legion season I started to feel alienated. Everyone went about their business without me. Even my close friends wouldn't call me to do stuff. I couldn't see that they were only men, and men forget. It really wasn't a big deal to me, but Natasha thought otherwise. She would say, "I think it's so messed that they don't invite you places." Because I was learning how to think the way others around me thought, trying to get my brain to see through other's eyes, I tried to look at things from a girl's perspective. For example, I began to care. I never cared about anything my friends were doing. Now I would wonder where are they? Why weren't they calling me? I want to say it is difficult thinking like a girl. Very difficult.

I walked in to Leominster Hospital finally time to have my eye surgery I had waited over a year for. The hope was that I would stop seeing two fuzzy objects and instead see one clear object. Immediately after the surgery I woke from my anesthesia. Everything was blurry. Something had gone wrong, I thought, but I remembered they had told me previous to surgery that when I woke up I would see blurry objects, I didn't panic. The doctor who conducted the surgery had told me this because my brain had to get used to the new alignment of my eyes.

The nurse entered and said I had to sit in the wheel chair to be taken out. I shook my head and told her the only way I would exit was on my own free will. I would walk out. There was no way I would get back in a wheel chair if I had the ability to walk. As I walked toward the exit, I felt the walls to ensure I was going the correct way. I'd bump into things on occasion, but finally made it to the exit and waited for my mother. It was blurry for the first few days. I remember watching TV, I was able to make out the images, I knew what was going on but it was a pain. I couldn't read until things began to clear up. But eventually I did end up seeing one when things remained still however when objects small in size, were moving at a high rate of speed, I would see two objects.

I placed posters on my walls just in front of my bed. Posters with inspirational messages. Every day when I woke, I would be reminded to work my hardest. One of the posters was Muhammad Ali standing over a man he'd just knocked out and it read *Impossible is nothing*. One read *The task ahead of you is never as great as the power within you.*

When I went to college I wanted to live on campus. I wanted to be a normal kid. So my parents and I decided I would live in a dormitory an hour away from home. I remember everything from my orientation. Like where the dinning common and convenience store was. My head began to fill with excitement as I looked at all the students who filled UMass' southwest section of campus.

I remember the night before I left to go to UMass, I was at a party. Natasha, of course didn't want to go. She didn't want to be surrounded by "Leominster" kids. I was missed her greatly and just wanted to be with her the night before I left, but I also wanted to see my friends. We were texting back and forth until finally I had enough. I had to see her. I drove to her house, rang the door bell and right when Natasha came out side said "I love you" and held her in my arms.

I honestly wasn't nervous about classes, honestly didn't even think about them. I was going to play baseball. I entered college to be a redshirt and play with the varsity baseball team at UMass. In fact, it was one of the first meetings I set up. I couldn't wait to talk to Coach Stone. I sat near him finally meeting the man who gave me this opportunity as he said, "Zach, adding your name will simply take up too much roster space."

I was absolutely heartbroken. Yet, I wasn't completely surprised. I was becoming clear that my first year in college would be very difficult. I vowed that I would train every day and work harder than I'd ever worked in my life. It wanted people to want me on their side again, not feel like I had to work to fit in.

Coach Stone still wanted me to be a part of the team. He offered me a position as a student manager. I would help out the team like a coach but without the pay or status. Basically, I was a free helper to the team. I was not on scholarship but rather recruited walk-on status. So for my work with the team they were not paying me. I tried the managerial gig for a couple of days, but with school and my wanting to train in order to play the following year, and the stress of recovering from a brain injury, I couldn't do it. I was beyond tired and all I wanted every afternoon was sleep. I finally went to coach and told him I couldn't do it anymore. He said, "That's too bad." But he understood why I couldn't. "I'm definitely trying out next year!" I said to him as I walked out the door for a nap.

Soon my training schedule consisted of going to the gym several hours daily; running on the elliptical machine, balancing, and extreme abs. I worked my ass off and had high expectations for winter break when I would go home and hit in the cages.

When I entered college I assumed that everyone would show sympathy and care about my story just as much as people back home. But I found a world where people only looked out for themselves. No one knew me or my story. They didn't know what I had been through. When I started to tell people my story at a party explaining to them why I wasn't drinking, people would say, "Aw, man that must of sucked," or "Glad to have ya back". But no one really cared. I wanted sincerity. But no one would sit and look me right in the eyes and care what I had to say; hear about the journey I was on and had been on. Back home this is the kind of attention I received. With these new people in my life, people who only knew me as the guy with a different walk and slower speech patterns, I realized I had to establish new relationships. It would be a long four years as I learned how to interact with these new people. It was as simple an adjustment as when I attended parties I would pray no one would bump into me to hard because I would lose my balance and fall for sure. I was afraid of becoming the one time star athlete turned into class clown.

Jon Hernandez is a good friend of mine. He's one of the closest friends I have ever had. We were pretty good friends in high school, but because of his girlfriend and my always off doing dumb shit, we didn't hangout that often. We became pretty good friends going into college. He was recruited by UMass to play football. I always thought it was funny that he was recruited by UMass for football and I for baseball, and neither of us knew where the other was going until Jon's graduation party.

Once classes started, Jon had somehow gotten pretty much the same schedule as me. We were with each other every second of every day. We walked to class together, sat in class together, and ate lunch together. The only time we were apart was when he had football. He would come over to hangout in my room. This was the start of a very long and meaningful friendship.

I used to sit in my room and think about what my friends from high school, who attended other colleges, were doing. I wondered if people forgot about me. I think I was concerned about what everyone else was doing because I was worried I wasn't as important as them. I had an identity back home. Here, I didn't recognize myself so I knew even less what others thought of me. In my hometown everyone showed their concern. Now, no one showed their concern. Even my old friends wouldn't call me or check in, they didn't show their compassion for me like they once had.

I quickly grew quite lonely. I couldn't see that this was what college and life as an adult was; people go off and do their own thing. You have to move on or be miserable. I didn't go off and do my own thing. I became miserable. I held onto the past, to high school and how awesome it was. I thought college was a speed bump in my life and that I would be with all my friends again after college, and things would return to 'normal.'

I woke on the first day of classes and said bye to my roommate, Dave. I grabbed something to eat then headed toward class with my map out to guide me. Entering the classroom, there was my roommate. At the same time we both exclaim, "You're in this class!" I grabbed a seat next to him then remembered I had to give the teacher a student services form in order to receive accommodations.

I walked to the front of the room and placed this form in front of the professor. "What is this?" he asked. I tell him that it is for accommodations for students with disabilities. He said in a very condescending tone, "Are you even going to be able to take this class?" I know that everyone in the small room heard him. I was so embarrassed. I started to justify my injury by telling him it's not that bad. As other professors began to find out what I went through, they joked with me and said they thought I had been coming to class drunk because my speech was so bad. This was the reason I avoided raising my hand to say something in class. That, and I wanted to avoid saying anything off-topic or stupid because I knew I could not fully process the information in time to make a valid statement.

I had the worst balance in the world. It wasn't even so much balance as it was the coordination. That winter the UMass campus got hit by storm after storm. There was ice everywhere. I was legitimately scared for my life to leave the comforts of my dorm. I didn't want to hit my head on the icy ground and risk further damage to my brain. My head was still tender at this point in my recovery.

I fell everywhere that winter. Not falls where I would softly land in the snow. My feet would slip out from under me and end up in the air over my head in some contorted way on the concrete. I would get up off the ground unable to breathe because I hit the ground so hard. People would ask me if I was okay, but I couldn't find the breath to answer them.

It seemed every time I left my dorm I would have a major fall at least once. I even tried to plan out my route to class around all possible dangers.

Jon was always by my side looking out for me. He knew how hard it was for me to walk on the ice. He was ready to catch me if I fell (even though many times he missed). He would constantly say, as we walked on a patch of ice, "Lean forward, lean forward." But I would end up falling the moment my concentration ran off to something else, like the hundreds of women walking past every five minutes.

A group of friends had this great idea to go roller-blading for this girl's Stacey's birthday. They asked my roommate and me to go. I owe Dave a lot; he did a lot for me that year. They wanted us to go and as they all drank I was, as usual, the driver. Soon after arriving I realized I couldn't roller blade. It didn't stop me from trying, but I couldn't even stand without falling. The moment I gained any balance I would stand and my feet would fly from under me.

If I leaned forward I could roll and look like I was doing something other than trying not to fall. Then one of my friends, Jenny, (who was my friend's girlfriend) rolled up behind me. She asked why I wasn't going fast. Startled by her noise I fell and landed right on my back. I looked up at her and said, "I can't roller blade. How about I hold on to you and you skate around the rink?" She agreed and that was how I got around the rink that night, holding onto her hips like a trailer hitched behind a truck.

Though I had friends who would did small things like this for me, I still felt alone. I would often stay in my room feeling alienated, like I had something better to do with my life than party and watch people drink every night. I didn't understand that this wasn't the only thing they did. They were just having fun, being college students, blowing off steam.

I also stayed in my room alone, often, so I could sleep. I would wake every day at 5:30 am and lie in bed until the gym opened at 7:00. I do not know why I woke at 5, but that's when my mental clock woke me. I would often lie in bed not wanting to get up, but I knew I had to begin the long road to living my dream. I worried what my body would look like if I skipped out on the gym for one day. I don't know why I had such an obsession with missing one gym day, I was just extremely dedicated to the gym.

Nightly, when everyone else went out or my roommate wasn't there, I would take out my weighted bat stowed underneath my bed, take swings and do drills to feel that burn in my forearms. I was hoping to get my bat speed back. Or I would take out a little Red Sox bat my parents gave me and work on my hand to eye coordination. It came with a stuffed little Red Sox ball and I would throw it up and take a swing using just my left arm. It might not seem like much, but every step I took toward reclaiming what I once was made me feel that much closer to normal.

The only way I made it through my freshman year of college was taking frequent naps. When I say the only way, I mean the ONLY way. My brain was so mentally exhausted from trying to figure out where I was going, what was going on in class, where my life was going, that I was mentally drained. I had to shut off my brain somehow. I took naps so often that my floor mates said I lived in a cave. I never had the lights on and I never had my shades up. It was always pitch black in my room. When everyone else would get together to go out or go eat, I would sleep. My roommate didn't mind, he knew I needed this in order to heal. He would try to come in as silently as he could to not disturb me. What I did not see was that this pattern was also the beginning of a depression I would suffer for much of my college career.

This is also how I became an outcast. I had a different schedule than everyone else, because unlike them, I needed to sleep constantly. When it was time to eat or I needed a walk I would go by myself or sometimes with Jon because it was too hard to get a bunch of people to conform to my schedule. Besides this is college right? Everyone only cares about themselves any way.

CHAPTER 5

DEPRESSION

As you would probably expect, I spiraled into a deep depression. I felt worthless and began to believe my life meant nothing. I could not play baseball, what I'd trained my entire life for and at what I'd become one of the best young players, the one release I had to blow off steam and help keep my mind off things. You're probably thinking, "Oh, that's no big deal. It's the same as if you'd hurt your arm or something like that." But keep in mind, in my daily life I couldn't do much of anything normal people do without second and sometimes third thought. I could not carry a tray with a drink on it because it would slide everywhere and spill on everything, I could not carry a cup of water without it splashing all over me and the floor, and I could not go up stairs very fast. I would hold up a whole line of people behind me and meanwhile feeling like a jackass. These may not seem like big situations or important details, but after it happens daily, from morning until night every single day for months and months, it adds up. It becomes a form of torture; I just wanted to be a normal kid and do things a normal kid does.

In my courses, I would study hard and fail my tests. It made no sense. My fellow classmates could go out every night, drink, stay up all hours and still get better grades than I. I stayed in almost every night, started papers a couple months before they were due, and I would get my paper back and receive a big D+. Yet, there were kids who I knew smoking weed and drinking all the time and receiving B's.

One day after I received another low test score, I finally had it and said to myself this can't be my life. I'm dumb. I can't do anything normal. I don't have any friends. I used to ask God all the time why me? I wondered why he would take out all of his anger out on me. I was a good kid, nice to everyone and tried to help others. So why did he have to come and take away my fun, happy life? I could not figure it out. Every day I spent hours thinking about my life and what it had become, how I had everything I could ever want; a great family, a great girlfriend, a great relationship with God, great friends and I was soaring in the sport I loved. It felt like I had lost everything. I felt distant from my family, felt like I had no friends and now God was even ignoring me.

Natasha was being extremely difficult and this added to my stress. She was upset because my life wasn't all about her any more. I paid more attention to myself and getting my life on track. It was both stressful and difficult to worry about her happiness in the midst of my own misery, and trying to dig myself out of this hole of depression at the same time. Instead of being able to call her and hangout with her and both of us finding comfort together, it became a huge production that had to have all the elements: do something she wanted to do, be with people she wanted to be with and find every outlet to her total happiness and satisfaction. My desire to be with her under those conditions became lessened as well.

I stayed in my room every night by myself to study and because I woke up early to lift. I really believed I was walking through a tunnel that had no light at the end. I was tired of working hard to see no results. The harder I worked, my goal of playing baseball seemed to move further away. There were moments that I really did not care if I lived or not. The struggle wasn't worth it. So I picked up a bottle of Jack Daniels that was in my roommate's fridge and held it in my lap.

I stared down the bottle neck into the liquor like it was the barrel of a colt .45. Because that's what it would be like, a bullet to my brain. I was not supposed to drink because I was still healing. Doctors said if I drank not just too much but even a little, I might forget how to walk, use my left hand, etc. One swig of this could destroy all of the progress I had made. But, it seemed rational. For just one night I could be happy. I wondered who would care if I lived or died.

As the bottle hit my lips, thoughts raced into my head. More memories than thoughts. Memories of the good times between Natasha and I, moments my family and I had, and memories of my friends flowed into my head faster than water through a busted dam. I couldn't do this. I worked too hard. I must be close to my goal of playing baseball again, and I knew if I destroyed myself in this dumb way, I'd hurt the people around me. My family, my girlfriend, and the friends that I still had left. I didn't need all these new people in my life any ways.

I slammed the bottle down and slapped myself in the face to wake up from this terrible dream. Except it wasn't a dream. I'd almost ruined my life and the lives of others with just one gulp of whiskey. I felt like a complete ass. This would, if carried out correctly, have been a terrible, selfish mistake.

At 7:30 am I woke to hit the gym, still ashamed of what had happened the previous night. When I arrived, my old friend Josh, who I played All-Stars with when I was 15 years old, was also there. We talked for a while and he started joining me every morning. He went to church a lot so he had many friends from church who lifted as well. He introduced me to some of his friends that he lifted with and he invited me in to his group of friends, in a way. Every morning we would get breakfast after the gym. We talked about things that mattered in today's economy, we laughed a lot with people staring at us being in such a good mood at nine in the morning. After all, they had the hangovers and we had just completed an intense workout. We also talked a lot about baseball. I finally felt like I belonged to a group. I looked forward to getting up at seven every day to hang out with these kids. Also, they helped me see God in a different way. I started going to Bible studies and enjoying what I would learn. I hoped if I repaired my relationship with God, he would help me and look out for me. Which I know he was there the night of my accident.

Finally, one year down in college! I was so excited for summer, I would get to hang out with all of my friends from high school. All my true, real friends that had stuck by my side during my recovery. Of course, I would also get to see Natasha. This made me happy to think that I'd be with her and she'd be with me but she was not as excited as I.

I thought I had rid myself of this depression. But I hadn't. At the beginning of the summer following my first year of college, I was harassed by a cop . . . and not for the first time. I'd been pulled over in the previous years for suspicion of drinking while driving numerous times. This particular time was the worst. We were in Saco, Maine, and they approached me for being in a vacant parking lot. The friends who I had followed drove away. Yet again, I was about to be harassed by another cop for no reason. They told me to step out of the car quicker than a New York minute. They began a physical sobriety test, which I failed miserably because of my coordination. I was able to do the balance test and pass, but it was the "walk a straight line" that got me arrested. Within minutes of wobbling off the straight line, the officer asked me to turn around and he slapped cuffs on me. He never read my rights and I was forced into the back of a cruiser. As I was being shoved into the back of the cruiser, I explained my situation to the officer. He told me to wait as he took each of my friends who were in my car aside and asked them why I was drunk. They both told him the same story separately about my physical condition, ut the officer didn't care.

The ride to the station was interesting as the cop pumped out Lil Wayne's "Lollipop". So I thought, this won't be that bad. Until I got shoved through the door of the basement of the police station. He then instructed me to get against the wall, which had a height measuring board. I said to myself, "Sweet! I'm going to be on like one of those shows with all the badass celebs to see which ones have the worst mug shot." I made sure I took the most badass mug shot ever, almost to mock him. He then took me to the area for fingerprinting. Then, I thought to myself, "Great I'm going to be on Americas Most Wanted." All this to eventually blow a 0.0 on the breathalyzer test.

"So you're arresting me for something I didn't do?" I asked. The officer said, "Wait until the piss man comes."

I remember being handcuffed to a pole and asking myself "The piss man????? Now he thinks I'm high. I have never done any drugs in my life." I passed all the tests I was given and I didn't even have to pee in a cup. But, I had to pee like a race horse because the cop was feeding me water the whole time. He wanted to make sure 'I went.' The cop made me pee (into a toilet) with the door open as he stared at my junk the entire time. All this for them to tell me I was telling the truth. As I walked out they told me they were dropping all charges.

That whole weekend I was unbelievably depressed. And to top things off I went hitting with my dad and sure enough, I was terrible. I sucked at everything. I couldn't hit, couldn't do normal routines, I had run-ins with cops and had to deal with their harassment, and I had no direction where my life was going. I had no idea what to do. Yet again, I wanted to drink to forget my sorrows. Then I laughed at the thought. Not again.

I had signs and posters that my friends made for me while I was in my coma in I.C.U. But I had had it. Enough of looking at the past. I tore down all signs and posters of my accident telling myself I had to move on.

I coached with Sid during the legion season all that summer. This was a great experience/opportunity to help get over baseball, or even better, to find an alternative to playing baseball. Except, it made me want to play even more, and all that crossed my mind was how I wished I was out there, how I should be out there. I worked with my uncle doing masonry work and after I would rush to the games.

I was absolutely miserable. This was not the salvation that I imagined. I couldn't wait for the season to end. I was happy Sid asked me to help coach, and I had a lot of fun. But I was sick of being depressed. I wanted to find an easy, quick way out.

Before the all-star game of 2008, I heard about baseball star Josh Hamilton. I heard about his struggles and how he found God. He would say with God by your side you can do anything you want. I watched eagerly during the homerun derby that year as he was a participant. He put on an absolute show and shattered the record for the number of first round home runs.

So I went home and did some detective work on Josh Hamilton. At this point in my life I had given up on baseball. Physically I wasn't near the shape I should be in for baseball, and I couldn't compete with the well-trained athletes who would be on the team my sophomore year. I'd considered when I returned to UMass I would try out for crew. I didn't want to believe Hamilton's story of his triumph over drugs was real. That someone could be out of baseball for several years and with the help of God he was able to return on top of his game. If it was real, that would mean another year of hard work and more added stress on my mind and body. If someone else could do it then that means that I am able to as well.

I looked up his story on espn.com and read about his hardships. He talked about how he would dream about the devil and the devil would try and corrupt him. How Hamilton would hit the devil down with a bat and he would get right back up. He then looked at his side and Jesus Christ was there fighting.

I decided this was what I needed to do. Not get mad at God, but to find the Lord and ask him for help and forgiveness. I turned my back out of anger. How could I be the kid everyone loved who in return cared about everyone and tried to be selfless and yet I was the kid that got into a car accident and had his whole life turned upside down? I kept asking God why. I would ask God to not let me wake up when I lay my head down to sleep. But just like Josh, he never granted that horrible wish.

Hamilton also said something on the lines of not asking God why, but asking him to help through your situation. That's what I needed to do.

I would tell my mom how excited I was about my new found inspiration . . . she would bring me back down to reality and say, "But Hun, drugs leave your body." She was referring to the ever-lasting effect, which one dreadful night had left me to deal with. Hamilton could shake his drug habit, detoxify, and retrain. My handicap was not drugs but the physical condition in which I was left. I couldn't detoxify from this. I'm not saying Hamilton had it easier, what I am saying is that I had hurt my brain so badly that I was lucky to do the things that I was doing, never mind fine tuning my brain and my body to play division one baseball.

I tried to get my body and mind right around the same time. I hoped this was the path to happiness. I visited a psychologist and a personal trainer near the end of that summer. I went to my personal trainer to find my career path. I went to the psychologist and found out that my girlfriend was causing most of my problems.

As I began to clear my head and set a course for my life and my healing, I started having problems with my girlfriend again. Most of the summer she didn't want to see me. I was neglected the entire summer. She blamed not wanting to be with me on the other people around me. For example, whomever I decided to hang out with that day. I was put in a position of having to choose between my friends from high school or Natasha. She didn't like any of them as they were all big drinkers. She would rather stay home than come out with me. It made me feel like shit.

One afternoon she said she was going to come over my house and lay out by the pool and swim. There was a cloud in the sky that afternoon. To her this was the equivalent of the sun not being out and she grew angry. A few days later I went over her house. I hadn't seen her since Saturday and it was Tuesday. Our absence from one another was ridiculous. We talked about why we didn't see one another more often for much of that day, and we both thought it was best if we took a break. I had no idea what 'a break' was. I asked my friends, even my parents, what are the rules to a break? My dad finally answered, "There are no rules!"

After my conversation with Natasha, I had enough. I went into the basement to get something to drink. Not a Coke or Pepsi. I was looking for something to ease the pain. Disaronno was in the fridge. I started feeling pretty good drink after drink, and for once I felt like 300 pounds was lifted from my back. I prayed that nothing bad would happen to me when I woke up in the morning, although maybe this time God would answer the prayer of my not waking up. A delayed granting of an earlier prayer. I went from the happiest kid on earth to a kid that drinks by himself in his basement. I had nothing in my life worth living for. I'm not ashamed or embarrassed to say that I thought about hurting myself. But would I ever do it? Absolutely not. Somewhere deep inside I knew there just had to be a light at the end of the tunnel, right?

CHAPTER 6

A NEW BEGINNING

I entered sophomore year with very low expectations. I expected nothing of myself, put no pressure on myself, and would be stress free. With this new attitude I thought, "I'm just going to keep to myself and not try and make a spectacle." Because I felt alienated I also thought, "They will all know who you are soon enough, and then they will all want to be your friends."

After we agreed that our break was over right before college, Natasha and I still weren't doing well. Everyone told me I could do better and I started to listen. One day I texted her I liked it when she would send text messages at night as I slept that read *You're the best boyfriend and I love you so much* and she reversed the meaning of my text and freaked out! She took it the wrong way, she made it seem like I was being sarcastic by saying I liked it when she would do those things. She said, "I'm sorry I don't call you during the day a lot but I'm busy too." That was it for me. I was sick of not being able to get close to her. She kept putting up walls and wouldn't let me get close to her. After all we'd been through those three years, I was sick of it. So I broke up with her through a text message because I was annoyed. I couldn't believe it ended the way it did. A stupid text out of frustration.

After the text message, I felt like an asshole. I drove to Westfield State College in Massachusetts to talk to her. By the time I arrived my pictures were already put away. She pretended to listen for three minutes and then told me to leave. For two months after that I fell into another deep depression. I thought I wanted her back and that I couldn't do better than her. So I drank . . . just like I had done before to get over my high school girlfriend, Toni. Derek and my Lil Bro came up and took me out. This would be the first time I got drunk since my accident. Better to say I got hammered. I drank way too much. I could barely walk. I ended up tripping down some stairs.

Then on another night, a Thursday night, Jeremy Yogel (my friend Matt Yogel's brother) yelled at the bartender, "Two Long Island ice tea's." We were at a bar in Amherst, Massachusetts. Jeremy was a great kid and always looked out for me. I decided I'd just sip on this one drink all night because of how strong it was. That is exactly what I did. It helped having my friends (Crush, Danny, Matt, and Jeremy) watch my every move, ready to pull the drink out of my hands if things looked like they were getting out of control. That was second time I drank in the span of two weeks, but I didn't care. I wasn't thinking about anything, finally!

I started to drink heavily again just to get my mind off her. During the semester, I got this sudden urge to drive to Washington D.C., to visit my friend Thomas taking my friend Mike along for the ride.

It was there that I realized I couldn't drink for several reasons. First, I was an alcoholic, I couldn't pace myself, I hadn't drank in three years yet I could still drink anyone under the table. Second, bad things would always happen to me. For example, I was absolutely wasted at a party while in D.C. We decided to walk home. We walked outside and walked down the stairs, right? Wrong. The stairs were made of concrete, all five or six of them, leading to a concrete sidewalk. I missed the first step. I fell straight to the bottom, my head turned into the railing. I almost cut off my ear; I smashed my head on the concrete. There was blood on the outside of my ear and it started bleeding on the inside. Thomas helped me walk back home because I was so drunk and disoriented from the fall. I was bleeding all over him but he assisted me the whole way.

They thought I was going to need stitches, but I could not go to a hospital because I was under age and drunk. So, Michelle, Thomas' girlfriend, helped stop the bleeding. She sat there for a good forty-five minutes to an hour holding a piece a cloth to help clot the bleeding. We had a serious heart-to-heart. It was there I realized where my life was headed if I followed a path that contained alcohol with this frequency. Thomas, one of my best friends said, "Look at yourself. You did this when Toni cheated on you, now you're doing it all over again." Then Michelle said something that has stuck with me, and will stick with me, forever.

She asked me why I drank and I said, "It's the only thing that makes me happy." She replied, "Look at yourself. Are you happy?" as I sat in pain with a bleeding ear.

On the way home, realizing how close to death I had come, I was quiet. I had just seen the bigger picture. I kept thinking to myself that I should be dead . . . . again. I'm not taking this, what, third chance at life, for granted. The doctors were afraid of me getting hit by a baseball with a helmet on, never mind falling several feet head first onto concrete with no helmet.

I had one expectation. That was get the perfect body. I was going to stop at nothing to achieve my goal. I loved my new goal because I didn't have to wait for anything to happen or for anything to fall into place. I could just go out and work as hard as possible. In the gym I had two goals: 1) get to 165 pounds, 2) get lean and obtain a six pack. I always wanted the perfect body, you know the washboard abs complete with the bulging biceps? I think the other reason for my obsession was so that I had somewhere to belong, to fit in. That's all I wanted, all I was trying to find.

I found in a forum on bodybuilding.com someone said it would work a lot better, and I would be a lot happier with myself, if I concentrated my goals separately. I decided to give it a shot. I was sick of being so skinny and small (148 lbs). I decided to bulk up and pretty much the only thing I did was eat. I would go to the dining commons five to six times a day. Classes got in the way a lot of the time so I'd bring a protein bar. I got my weight up to 168. In two and half months, I gained that much weight and I thought I was so big . . . . it felt great. Then I noticed I had gained a great deal of fat. It was time to start the cutting cycle.

Around this time I met my friend David Cozzo. He was from Miami and played football with Jon. I think I was drawn to him because he was different from any one that I have ever met. I can explain who Cozzo is in a very few words. A good looking kid who thinks that life is a movie and the camera's always on him. I loved hanging out with Cozzo and he ended up becoming one of my good friends. Our dining common was open late. I would go often with Cozzo and Jon to eat as much as I could for my bulking phase.

I loved lifting and decided to take it more seriously. I used Natasha as motivation. I used to do curls in the mirror at the gym and say to myself, once Natasha sees me she's going to want me back. But, soon my friend

Jon would introduce me to a girl he knew from back home, attending UMass, and she was absolutely perfect. You will hear that story later.

I went on bodybuilding.com and spent much time in the forums asking questions. Or often, even better, I would just read the forums instead of asking questions. A lot of the muscle-heads would make fun and say things like, "Go do some research." Well, what did the brilliant ones think I was doing? I still couldn't find the exact routine that worked for me. My friend Joe was a personal trainer. He suggested I do short intervals of high intensity. He said, "Remember, you want the body of a sprinter not of a long distance runner." This stuck with me and it's true sprinters are jacked and have nice bodies. Long distances runners not so much. I discovered it was not just high intensity, but what I wanted was called high intensity interval training or HIIT.

Jon (who had the perfect body) was a running back for UMass. He said, "You need to do sprints. It does something with your abs. It helps them come out." I asked my dad about this and he simply asked, "Have you ever seen a fat sprinter?" All I needed now was to incorporate HIIT with sprinting. Which was pretty simple because I would sprint on the treadmill then walk for a minute after.

Because I had to learn how to run all over again, I first started to sprint weird. I limped and my left arm wouldn't move correctly. I held it tight to the side of my body because when I first jogged after rehab I had no strength in my arm, so it would flail in the air. This was the only way I could control it. Starting out, I had to concentrate staying straight on the treadmill because my left leg would kick out at random times. On a treadmill you must stay straight. Well, my foot would always kick out just enough so that half of my foot would be on the moving track and the other half on the part that wasn't moving. It would twist me and I would trip, barely able to grab onto the handles before I fell. I had to hold on for dear life and try to move my feet as fast as I could to catch up to the speed of the treadmill. I couldn't run on my toes, so you would hear a gentle landing when my right foot touched followed by a big bang with my left foot. I looked like an idiot. Because I was in Amherst, Massachusetts, away from home, nobody knew why I ran like that. They just thought something was wrong with me. Everyone would stare at me when I ran. When I messed up and would almost fall off or trip *everyone* would see it. People were so rude they would just shake their heads as if to say I shouldn't have had the treadmill so fast. But I was trying to re-train my brain how to sprint. They just didn't get it.

I could run on the speed of ten and it looked borderline graceful. Just when I thought I was finally past the worst, probably the most embarrassing thing that can happen at the gym happened. I was on the treadmill warming up on 7.5 when the treadmill made a weird noise and all of sudden sped up. I tried to run as fast as I could and stayed with it for awhile, but my left leg got fatigued. I caught the edge of the track and the sideboard. My foot got twisted and once again I held on for dear life. I held on to the treadmill and my feet just dragged behind and this machine was flying. I tried to get out of this situation without injury, so I tried the commando roll to get off. As I hit the mat to roll, it grabbed me and shot me off the back, and I ended up on the ground. Of course people are going to talk to you to make you feel better; "Are you ok?" or "I heard it make a weird sound too." But I was so embarrassed. It didn't keep me from finding another treadmill and getting my work in.

Jon always watched out for me and I knew he had my back when shit hit the fan. He played football for UMass now, but still made time to hang out. We actually hung out a lot, and thanks to him I am the man I am today. He helped me get back on my feet after the relationship with Natasha. He was like, "We're gonna get you organized, and were gonna find you a good girl." Then one day after Jon promised that he would find me a girl, he bumped into a sweet Guatemalan girl from back home named Dianne in the dining common. He was friends with her brother for a long time and didn't even know she attended UMass. He showed me her profile on Facebook and just like that I fell in love.

I was always this kid who was way too nice. I have gotten walked all over because of it. People took advantage of my generosity. Jon knew this and he knew that after the accident I had to learn everything all over again. Even simple things like being "a man." I know this sounds funny, but it's true. I was completely lost hanging out with the wrong kids, kids that didn't actually care about me as much as I thought they did. He told me it was time that I "man up" and stop feeling sorry for myself. From then on I hung out with Jon. He showed me by example to be friendly to everyone, or give them the occasional head bob that meant 'what's up', but to only let close friends or 'good people' close to me. I stopped caring about what others thought; stopped caring whether they liked me or not. Because of those lessons Jon taught me, the reminders of who I was, I love who I am today.

That was the first step in getting Dianne to be my girl. I had to become a man all over again. When I would text Dianne, Jon would tell me exactly what to say. He'd be like 'say this' and I would write how I needed to see her and then read it over and over, then he would say 'man up' and I would hit the send button. The only problem was that I had gained interest in the busiest girl in the world. It seemed like she never had time to spend with me. I grew frustrated, but it wasn't the end of the world. There were plenty of girls out there.

Jon came to live with me during winter break. His family had moved to Florida so he had nowhere to go. He was going through a lot between money problems, his girlfriend, and not having a place to call home. So, I wanted to help him just like he took care of me. I would always pay whenever he needed a spot, and he would offer to pay for me whenever he had the money. I knew he had my back no matter what type of shit I got into, and he was going to help me by just being a good friend. Jon also pushed me in the gym. He helped me do things I thought I couldn't. For example, I did not think that I could bench (using the bar, not dumbbells) because my left arm was so weak. But he spotted me once and pushed me after I would have long ago stopped. I put up 135 pounds twelve times.

Also, during winter break, I was forced to have surgery on my big right toe to get rid of a chronic ingrown toe nail I had. This left me with some problems in the gym but it wouldn't stop me from working hard, the next day I could I was on the treadmill running.

No matter how big I got, I still wasn't as big or as cut as Jon. He was my motivation. That whole winter he made me eat better and he made me work out harder. So much so I was doing sprints because now I did not look like an idiot any more, and I actually felt semi-graceful. My goal was now to try and get as lean as possible. I didn't have the genetics to get as big as Jon, but I did have genetics to get lean. It seemed like I might actually make it. I thought perhaps I might be able to play ball next year. No one believed in me. Even my parents told me it was time to move on. They were proud that in appearance I had moved on, but that was just an act for people. Deep inside, I believed I could make it The whole year I kept trying to convince myself out of actually going through with the tryout. I convinced myself not to be disappointed by finding the littlest things that I couldn't do and saying, "Well, I'm not going to play baseball if I can't do this."

I didn't want to believe in myself because I was afraid in letting down myself. I pretended to not care but deep inside I really did care. It was the only thing I would think about. I stayed up late one night and watched *Rookie of the Year*. He persevered over everything and overcame the odds. I wanted to have a similar story, and I knew wouldn't give up.

I ran on the treadmill as much as I could that winter during our holiday break. Because of the way my left foot landed on the treadmill, the back of my knee began to hurt. I could tell it was the same place it hurt when I was re-learning to walk. It was also the same type of pain I felt during that period. This meant my leg was slightly hyper-extending (my knee was bending backward). While the pain was not excruciating, it hurt constantly. Whether I was walking or running, the pain was there. The only way to rid myself of this annoying pain was to keep running, which only made it hurt more. But, the only way to make it stronger was to run. I was doing Jon's football workout, involving hills. In a moment of reflection, I gave myself kudos. I could now run fast up-hill on a treadmill when last year I couldn't even jog on one.

The winter break passed and I had one major motivation for returning to school . . . Dianne. Although I shouldn't of been so excited. She never returned my phone calls or texts and she went to Guatemala for two weeks of the break.

When I went back to school I had one objective on my mind . . . . get a nice body. I figured this would solve my problems; I would get more self confidence in myself, girls would want me, this would help me play baseball again, and I could hopefully avoid yet another bout with depression. By running every day it helped my brain get right. I could see improvements. For example, the first weekend back from break I went to a party. I did not drink, but Jon did and when Jon drinks . . . Jon likes to dance. He and I had about six girls dancing with us. I could actually keep the beat, like I actually had rhythm. I was getting complements left and right. It was great to finally after three years be the center of entertainment.

The next morning I woke at 6 a.m. as I usually did, but I did not have to go to the gym because it was Saturday. I surprisingly found myself thinking of a girl. (OK, not so surprising.) But I wasn't thinking

of Dianne, and not Natasha, but Toni. My first girlfriend in high
school, my first love. That was the happiest I had ever been. I played
baseball all day, went to the gym, and then would just hang out with
Toni all night. It was the first and only time I had my whole life figured
out. After arguing back and forth with myself, I decided I only wanted
to be with her again because of those memories, and the hope that I
might play ball again.

It seemed every day a new girl would be introduced in my life. The
whole Dianne thing was pretty much over. If she didn't want to see
me, I couldn't make her. But, I was caught between a couple of girls.
Natasha (she started talking to me again by instant messages here and
there), and there was my sweet Williana. Williana was a girl I met in
my basic writing class freshman year. We became really good friends. I
loved hanging out with her and I could tell she had fun being with me.
But, that's all we were. Friends. And I didn't want to ruin that with a
relationship. The funny thing was I really didn't have a shot with any
of these girls. But I thought I did have a chance because the way girls
would lead me on. They would text me that they missed me or say they
wanted to hang out with me. I guess I don't know if I did or not but
they were extremely good at leading me on, whether they meant to or
not.

Oh yes, Natasha. She started instant messaging me again at the
beginning of the spring semester. I'd decided that if she IM's me, we
have a chance to get back together. One evening Jon and me were in
my room watching T.V., and there's a new IM.

"Yup, that is Natasha," I said to Jon. She said she missed talking
to me and wanted to know how I was. Then she asked, "Sooo are you
seeing anyone?" I answered back, "No, I have a lot of good friends that
are girls, but can't go through something that emotional again." She
said the same thing and we just talked about everyday things. But, she
had me thinking. Could it be that this was meant to happen? A break
was all we needed.

But if she hadn't changed, then I couldn't . . . I did not want . . . to
go back to that. I was so confused. I didn't have a care in the world. I
went to the gym and concentrated on school and smiled knowing God
had something good in store for me.

CHAPTER 7

OPTIMISM

My life was turning around this time. I didn't want to believe it because just like so many times before I was let down. Now, I couldn't sleep at night because I was so excited about life. I thanked God every five minutes during the day. I couldn't be happier. I know this might not make sense, but I was so excited about my new life it was almost like I couldn't relax. I was always thinking about something whether girls, baseball, school, or my body. I couldn't sleep at night with thoughts spinning through my head. Then sometimes I would just laugh at myself. As if to say, "This can't be happening . . . . look at my life . . . . absolutely incredible." If someone was looking at my life and didn't already know everything that happened to me, they would just be in awe of everything I had already accomplished.

I made sure to take time out of my day to encourage others. I would be online reading Facebook updates or away messages and these would read things like: "o I hate my life" or "FML" (fuck my life). Even if I hadn't talked to these friends in a long time I would IM them and tell them to keep their heads up, that they have a good family and good friends. Maybe I would just give them someone to talk to. Sometimes that's all people need.

There was a reason God kept me on this earth. I started considering the reasons I survived. I thought maybe he kept me alive so that I could help my friends, or maybe to make everyone's day that much better as they see me walk in the room with my big, dumb, goofy smile.

But, I was still hoping that some way, somehow, he would incorporate baseball in my life. I couldn't let go. It was in my veins. But if I didn't play baseball again, I had to believe there was a reason. I still hoped my niche in the world was to play baseball and to spread the message that with a little faith, hard work, and determination, impossible is actually nothing, that you can accomplish anything you want as long as you want it bad enough. Kind of like Josh Hamilton, but my story was a little bit different. Everyone's story is always a little different.

I thought that maybe making a name in baseball I could get people to read and listen to my story. Because baseball would get my name out there, everyone would see what I accomplished and want to hear about the path I took to get what I achieved. I wrote most of my story in college in my dorm room, during my recovery, when I had nothing to do or instead of going out. I wrote this story as though I was destined to play, and that God would one day give me the chance to prove to a world of doubters that you can accomplish anything you want no matter the odds.

Writing my story in college was very therapeutic. I would go out to a party or to the dining common and see all these Division One athletes and think, "They all think they are the best right now, but wait till they hear my story. They think they have accomplished a lot . . . awards and whatnot . . . . well that's nothing compared to what I have already achieved."

My message was simple: you never have to face anything alone. There is no need to have fear, there is no reason to be scared, because you are never really alone. God will always be by your side. Yeah, sometimes the devil may get his hands on you, but God is going to be there with you all the way.

I then met Ambar. Her old roommate, Jen (a friend of mine), and Wilianna were in my math class. They would help me with the assignments. After having to re-learn math I had no chance of learning *linear equations*. Ambar would come over to Jenn's side of the room and talk to me. She would laugh and giggle and would get me to write her papers. She would pay me because she hated writing and I was good at it.

One of my many days of thinking *screw girls, I just want to focus on my grades and my body*, I got text from Ambar. It read . . . "loser!!!" I replied back something like, "wow, didn't we already go over this the other night." The previous night we texted back and forth playing this ridiculous game where we called each other loser over and over. Then she texted back . . . "lol it means I like u a lot!!!" I showed my friend Jon and he knew what

I felt. He was happy for me. I thought, "Man that was easy . . . I wasn't trying nor looking for a girl and yet one likes me." I was so excited. She seemed like a really good girl. And maybe I liked her too. Jon and I went to a party in Westfield. Natasha went to Westfield State College, a very small school. There was a good chance I was going to see her. As I walk in the room, there she was. It's almost like I knew she was there before I actually saw her. The same smile I fell in love with, the same smile that makes me smile just seeing it. How do you not notice a smile so bright that you have to squint to see where the shine came from?

She was easily, in my eyes, the most beautiful girl on the planet. I saw her and said, "Oh boy, you just fell back in love." Yet, I thought I had just started something with Ambar. Looks aren't everything and it would have to come down to who treated me better. Natasha will always have a leg up on the competition . . . there was something still there between us; was it love? We barely even talked at the party and she barely showed me attention. Yet, I still sought her out to talk. Why? I do not know. I just felt like I owed it to her to try to make it work.

I thought I was caught in a love triangle. I was so confused. Yet, I loved every minute of it. I thought my life was making a turn for the better, and on top of the girls, my body was showing signs that it was actually going to look the way I wanted by summer. With all the hard work trying to get my body right, all the muscle fibers and nerves in my body were finally making new connections! My baseball skills could return if my body worked as it did prior to my accident.

My toe still hurt from the surgery. It hurt every time something touched it, stepped on it, or just when I walked. I called the Doctor and set up an appointment to meet with him. It was infected and I was constantly in pain . . . again. I had to keep at it (in the gym), had to keep training if I one day wanted to play baseball again. I had finally had too much. My body told me it needed a break from running. I still wanted to do the HIIT workouts though. So I created a bike workout and incorporated HIIT. The workout went something like this:

> 2mins at 110 RPM HI
> 3mins at 50-65 RPM LI
> 2mins at 110 RPM HI
> 3mins AT 50-65 RPM LI
> Repeat cycle 2-3 times

I thought it was a good workout and I was seeing results and fast. My knee had been hurting as well and this was the best way to get results and let my body rest. The best thing about this routine was I could actually pedal the bike. When I was first out of the accident, my left leg could not keep up with the pedal. I would pedal fast, but then it would reach a point that my right leg would take over and go way to fast and my left leg would try to pedal, but couldn't keep up. I looked like a complete jackass. People must have thought, "Does this kid really not know how to pedal a stationary bicycle?" The answer was NO! I don't.

I started getting involved in personal training and created for my friend Jenny a workout. I was beginning to consider this my career path. I wanted my future to have something to do with a gym or health club. After all I'd experienced in life, this was the one constant place for me. I could always go to the gym to get away and the gym saved, or improved, my quality of life. Remember, doctors said that if I was not in as good of shape as I was, I would not have survived the crash.

Oh my God, I was so confused by girls . . . all the time. But I guess this comes with the territory of having a brain injury. Girls can lead you on so easily if you're a man with a brain injury. Even if you're a man without a brain injury they can confuse you, but factor in the brain injury and I was a lost soul.

I thought that Natasha was the only girl that I was going to feel this crazy about so I would wait for her until she tells me that we are done for good. I texted her and said, "I wanna have dinner with you ova break." She didn't reply until the next day. She wrote a long text that went something like this . . . "hey! Srry I didn't get bak to you! I am busy all break, I have observation hours tues-thurs but im free on the weekends." I replied "haha that's alright just let me know when you are free."

"Alright! I will."

I thought I was in the perfect position, I thought I was right where I wanted to be. I went to Tennessee, to visit my aunt Tammy and my uncle Ed for spring break, and life was good, absolutely no worries. I went with my dad and my brother Jon (not Mike or Derek). Jon and I made a vow not to talk about girls. Women always came up in our conversations. It was great to get away from everything; no one knew where we were. Dead to the world, I thought to myself. I rode a horse, I saw hicks, cows, pigs, and minihorses. I fell in love with the minihorses. They were so cute. My uncle said he could help me get one for free and start my own minihorse farm. I thought about life in the country, and thought that Tennessee would be a nice place to live. I, for some reason, started to picture myself in the countryside. My uncle was retired special forces, so this began to make me think maybe I should join the military, save up money. Then when I am ready to settle down, move to Tennessee. Oh man! I needed to stop changing my mind about everything. I was so excited about the future my mind was going a mile a minute.

When I returned from Tennessee, I went to the batting cages to help Dad with his team. After practice, I saw the man who is one of the reasons for my story being recorded, Sid. He couldn't believe how far I had come. It was a year since I had seen him last. All he could talk about was my progress and how good I looked. He went on and on about how I should write a book and how I should be a motivational speaker. It was hard to hide from him that I was currently writing my story. On the way out he said, "Alright, Zach I'll see you tomorrow . . . and I'll have my plan for you to make a million dollars soon!" I laughed.

I was still hoping to play baseball, at least in college.

One issue scared me as I hit with Jon in the cage after practice. I was still seeing double with small fast moving objects, which is what a baseball is coming out of the machine. I still made solid contact and hit doubles in the power alleys of any ball park. I could not let seeing double discourage me. I had to keep my head up to achieve greatness. My temperament had changed from only a year ago when I would have been swearing or yelling at nothing but expressing pure anger. This time I was cool and calm.

The next day, I stumbled into a tattoo parlor. All I wanted was prices on tattoo ideas. I've wanted to get my mom's name somewhere. Then, Andy said, "If you wait like 15 minutes I'll get you." So that was that. I walked in to look at prices and I walk out with MARYANN inked on my chest. "This is her mother's day present," I said to Jon. I hid it for a couple weeks till she saw me without my shirt on. If I feel strongly about something, there is no hesitation on tattoo's for me. That is why I only have my mother's name, my grandfather's dog tags, and my savior's cross tattooed on my body at this point. I promised God that I would get one on my back that read *animus deus*, Which means "soul of God" in Latin if I played baseball in college.

My adventures into tattoos began when I was about ten. I saw some guys in my town with tattoos of crosses and people I admired with a big cross tatted on their arm. I always wanted a tattoo as long as I can remember. When I turned eighteen, I went to Florida and I got a tattoo of a cross on my arm. I became obsessed. I loved them! But there was something bigger than the look that got me to keep inking myself.

After the accident, I felt like I owed God and this was the best way to repay him, besides being a good person. I felt like I owed him for saving my life that night and giving me this brand new life. Yes, I had to start from scratch, and learn how to do everything over again, but it was worth it. I was living, right?

The same went for my mother. There was no way I could repay her for the love that she has shown me. The unconditional love that she showed me every night I was in the I.C.U. or rehab. Her love that she gave inspired me to heal and not let her down, I just couldn't do that. The only way I could think to repay her was be to brand myself forever hers. My mother was my guardian angel, my savior, the only women that has, no matter what, stayed true to me.

A couple days later, still on our spring break, Jon, his cousin Xavier (Puky), and I went to a party in town. We were arguing with these girls as they left the house to not drive because they were too drunk. As we left the party walking a different direction, I heard the screeching of tires, and saw a black Sedan going 35-40mph down a street where that was twice the speed limit. We began to walk on Main Street from the party to my car that was parked on the side of the road. We looked toward the road to see what all the noise was about. The Sedan hit a curb at an angle, went airborne and flew into a telephone pole. Since it hit the curb on an angle it tilted the car slightly, which made the car hit the telephone pole, flip and land on its roof. The car must have gotten fifteen feet of air. It was something that you would see in the movies. Then the car slid several feet. Puky and Jon yelled call 911! I was in absolute shock as I walked toward the car in mid-slide. I was so in shock with what I had just witnessed that it was almost like I forgotten how to run.

We felt it as though it was imperative to pull the girls out of the car; the way the car was flipped, if it had caught fire the girls would have no chance in hell to get out. Jon, Puky, and I all grabbed what we could of the girls and pulled them out one by one. Jon and I pulled ours out first. I dragged the young woman to safety by grabbing her torso and dragging her feet. She tried to walk, but couldn't. She just stumbled everywhere. Although, the driver was still in the car, Jon and I knew that we had to get the girls already out as far away from the car as possible.

Puky ran to the driver's side. I had already looked and couldn't find a way to get to her because the window was still intact. I thought about kicking in the window, but thought she was probably on the other side near the passenger window trying to get out. Puky saw the driver had actually gotten tangled in the seat belt. She couldn't have released herself. Thank God she wore her seat belt or she would likely be dead. The cops were on their way and the three girls yelled at us to leave. "You guys need to leave, the cops can't find you guys or you'll get in trouble. "I immediately thought of Jon. Even though he had turned twenty-one that week, he was a Division 1 AA football player. Cops like to catch a kid like that doing something wrong.

It makes me angry people don't learn from my mistake. They don't understand what I had to go through day in and day out just to be a normal again. One of the girls told me to be careful and that I shouldn't be driving. I can't stand people who try to lecture me on how to be safe when they, themselves, don't know how to get home safely. They could barely stand when we were in the party; the driver alone must of stumbled and fell at least six times.

This experience touched me in a way similar to how my accident did. My accident changed my life for obvious reasons, but this beat it into my brain that alcohol and vehicles do not mix. This experience changed my life. We could have pulled dead bodies out of the car. Everything I have seen and witnessed in my short life has made me mature extremely fast. Think about it; at 20 years old I thought I would be pulling my dead friends out of a car. I know soldiers have to do things like this on occasion, but they are in a warzone or on a battlefield. They have some kind of mindset readied that they might have to do something like this. And even for them, as prepared as they might be, it is never easy. Walking home from a party? You can probably put yourself in my shoes feeling shock and knowing how unprepared I was.

When I got back to UMass after spring break I received surprising news. The University of Massachusetts was to cut their baseball team entirely next year. My friend Audrey told me this at dinner one night. I was so angry. When I was home over break I had gone to the cages and done pretty well. I still needed much improvement, but there was potential. I was just starting to get my confidence back with baseball when I find out that I can't tryout because they were cutting the team. I was so frustrated I did the only thing that could get me in a better mood; I went to the gym. As I was at the gym I ran extremely well. Except my left foot kept making a slapping noise on every stride. It was unbelievably loud! The person next to me had to find another treadmill that wasn't next to a noisy neighbor. But, my strides were perfect . . . I had almost no limp!

While I was at the gym I was so mad, I punished myself. I did this out of because I did not get my chance to try out for the team. I took out all of my anger and frustration on myself. All my lifts I did until failure. But, my chest hurt so bad during and after and I was sure tomorrow it would hurt even more. As I was at the gym, I developed a plan of a couple different scenarios. See, the thing that pissed me off the most was that I couldn't even give baseball tryouts a shot. Also, I liked UMass, I liked the people, my major, and the set-up, but they had no baseball now. I should have known it was going to be harder than what I had planned. It always is. That's one thing I've learned for certain.

One of my new scenarios was go to UMass Amherst for the fall semester and transfer to UMass Lowell. Maybe tryout for the club team, but I doubted they would want someone only there for half the year. I picked UMass Lowell because right after rehab I received a letter from the coach of UMass Lowell saying regardless of what happened to me or where I was currently, he wanted me to play for him. He was a really good guy and that drew me to him. I also chose UMass Lowell because I was trying to find out if they had journalism and I stumbled upon a major that was even better. Nutritional Science. It was perfect . . . something that interested me and could help if I did become a personal trainer.

I thought, even though very selfish of a thought, that the program getting cut at UMass Amherst was cut by God for me. God wanted me to be able to play baseball, but also set up my career. That night I got on my computer and wrote an email to Coach Stone asking about what I had heard. This was his response:

Zach,

The rumors about the future of UMass Baseball are just that, rumors at this point. I think that we should know something definite within the next two weeks.

Coach Stone

I hadn't talked to Natasha since spring break when she ditched me for dinner and said she "forgot." I said fuck her; I'm just going to have fun. The next weekend her best friend Annie came up to UMass. Annie and I go way back . . . . all the way back to an 8th grade crush we had on each other, but that's neither here nor there. She came up and we had a great deal of fun. I stayed completely sober, but Jon and I made sure Annie and her friends Kara and Kelly had fun that night. They laughed the whole time. I believe Annie told Natasha how much fun she had with us as that Sunday her away message for AIM was this:

I'm weak, its true
Cause I'm afraid to know the answer
Do you want me too?
Cause my heart keeps falling
I've waited all my life to cross this line
To the only thing that's true

I don't know this message was directed at me. But if that doesn't lead you on, please tell me what does? I was starting to get very angry. I felt like saying to her if you want me then tell me, I'm willing to give you another chance. If not, stop leading me on. Girls . . . .

I had baseball back in my life as small a dose as it was; I was working incredibly hard to get a nice body for summer, and returned to my mantra: "I'm going to have a great time and make sure everyone else does too, no matter where I go."

After spring break I was impressed with how I picked up a bat and started to smash line drives. I had two really good hits off the machine that would have been easy doubles anywhere. But I also swung and missed a lot, though I did not stress because I knew it was just my eyes needing to focus. I also was impressed with how I played catch with Jon, but there was room for improvement. I needed to progress a great deal to roam the outfield for any team. When I came home from spring break I brought my glove to UMass and played catch with myself, like I had done freshman year in my dorm room. I would lie in my bed, with my headphones on, and throw the ball up and catch (without two hands). I did this to work on hand-eye coordination. I got really good, which only took a week. I think the ability to learn new things quickly came from all the HI running I did. I believe this made my brain think faster. My doctor believes otherwise, She believes that it was more my strong desire and motivation that helped me think faster and learn new things rather than how fast I would run. I still believe that this helped me though.

Once I got really good and my hand instinctively went to the ball to catch it I did something that may sound dangerous, I whipped the ball against the cement ceiling. The ball would bounce off extremely fast and force me to react even faster. I'm not going to lie; there may have been a couple of times that the ball bounced off the walls and hit me. In fact, it hit me in the chest or face almost 90% of the time. I swear the ball sped up after it made contact with the wall. I quickly learned I had to react faster, and this made me better.

I thought for sure I would be able to play baseball again sooner than I once believed. I could see daily small improvements in every aspect to be a good player again. I didn't feel as big of an idiot with all these promises I'd made. All the newspapers and especially the magazine that put me on the cover where I'd promised I'd play again, I could not let them down. I believe the direct quote was, "I want to go Division One. Because I know I can. And I'm gonna." I began to believe I could stop living the life of a letdown. I was the happiest kid, and excited for what was about to come.

My whole life it seemed things had not gone the way I'd envisioned. I always fell just short of where I knew I could land. I didn't make the 12 yr-old All-Star team when I was 11, but yet ended up being the only freshman to play varsity. I was often harassed by cops. Hell, once ll my clothes were stolen out of the dryer the previous year in college. That same week someone had a flat tire, jacked up my car and switched their flat with my good tire. But all you can do is laugh. Right? People are pricks. How pathetic is your life if you'd do that to someone else.

Brush it off, Zach. Life is good

CHAPTER 8

TRANSFORMATION

H ere begins my total body transformation near the end of my sophomore year in college. My mind, body, and mentality were all changing

When I was going through my mind and body transformation, I took a break from baseball. After the break; working began to be fun and not frustrating. I hadn't felt this way since before my accident. I looked forward to playing catch alone after every one of my classes. I didn't have to work to focus on the ball going into the glove every time I threw it in the air. I no longer had to strain my arm trying to direct it to the ball to catch it which left a burning sensation in my shoulder. This meant that the nerves were coming back, or this is what I'm told by my mother.

I began to develop feelings for Annie, Natasha's best friend. But I felt I needed something to help me out when Jon, Annie, and I would hangout. Every girl wanted him when they began to drink a little. He was the Division 1 football player with the perfect body. Every girl thought he was cute. Later I found out she really was attracted to him . . . even sober. Again I found myself confused because Annie would hit me up and text me to see what I was doing. She knew I would be with Jon. At the time I believed she liked me. You can get tricked easily after you have had a brain injury. It sucked, but I figured it out over time.

I began to grow this mentality of; if you're not with me you're against me. I would do my thing and if you didn't like, you could go screw. I would hang out with who I wanted when I wanted and nobody would tell me different. All these people around me only cared about themselves at this school. It was ridiculous. Maybe in retrospect it wasn't that bad, but at the time I hated everyone who wouldn't say hi to me. I had to learn that strangers don't say 'hi' to people they don't know. I always did. Also, I came from a city where everyone knew who I was and they would always say hello. But no one knew me here. I didn't understand that people only greet you when they actually know you.

Natasha was mostly irrelevant at this point in my life. If she didn't want to get back with me then that was her loss. I was working to be somebody. With this story and what I have done to where I'm at, I'm going somewhere. I felt God had my back and as long as I worked hard, I would get where I wanted. I too, felt that God had a plan for me with women too. It was time to relax and concentrate on me (baseball, my book and my body) and let God's plan take its course. If all else failed I always had match.com.

At the same time I felt that if Natasha wanted another chance I owed her at least that for everything she did for me. If she wanted another chance I planned to tell her, "Let's start on a clean slate, and everything we did to each other before doesn't matter." For example when I got in the accident I hurt her, I put her through a lot. When she wouldn't give me a second chance, she hurt me.

Then Jon got me into the music of Tupac Shakur, or 2pac. I related because 2pac talked about struggle, and I related his struggle to mine. Even though I never sold rocks or anything like that, I still related to the lyrics. My struggle was just a different one than 2pac's. In Thugz Mansion he sings, "No one sees my struggle, they only see the trouble, not knowing it's hard to carry on when no one loves you." This was my situation. Everyone would see me walk around campus with a limp, having trouble balancing, but no one knew why I was messed up. They assumed I had something wrong with me and that I was a weird kid. I didn't think I had any friends. I don't know why I thought this, but I did. So when he says that it's hard to carry on when no one loves you I felt my believed lack of friends was exactly what he was talking about.

Jon wasn't going to let me slack off. He was on me all the time. He would call me to go play catch in between classes. When he stayed with me for the summer, we hit all the time and played catch every day. I helped him with football and he helped me with baseball.

Another way Jon kept me (indirectly) working hard is that Jon's body was absolutely perfect. I would look at myself in the mirror and think, "My arms are starting to fill out and my stomach is near flat." Then Jon would come over to my dorm room on our way to eat, but we went in the bathroom first to take a piss. We would, just joking around, show off our stomachs in the mirror. He said, "You lost your belly, but damn just that little tiny bit of fat." This made me work even harder at the gym. Jon would always say to me, "Kid, you were in an accident, you gotta remember that." I would reply, "It's forgetting that has gotten me this far."

Baseball was looking good. When I went home for spring break I hit the crap out of the ball when Jon threw it to me, but off the machine was a different story. I believed that I could do it eventually. I just had to be patient . . . again. I hate that word; wait,wait,wait. I was sick of waiting. Those two line drives I hit off the machine were proof with a little practice I could do this.

YOU MUST LOOK AT THE SMALL ACHIEVEMENTS, THEY HELP GIVE YOU CONFIDENCE.

My arm grew better and better at going right to the ball for a catch. I could throw the ball up (when standing) and just use my peripheral vision to catch the ball. The biggest obstacle, the one thing I had to be able to do, run, had improved beyond expectation. I could run on 8 mph for two minutes and 9 or 9.5 mph for a minute and a half.

My day consisted of breakfast as early as I could (eating kick starts your metabolism), class, home work. If I had no homework I would throw the ball and catch it using my left hand to practice hand-eye coordination with the television tuned to FCS (Fox College Sports). I would critique hitter's swings and take note of any mental mistake they would make to stay up on my knowledge of baseball. Often I would say something to Jon like, "He got a great jump, or he pulled his head and that's why he popped up." The commentators would say the same exact thing, almost as if they had heard me.

I would eat again. I tried to eat as many times as I could, but small meals. After three hours your metabolism starts to slow down. So I tried to eat every two and half or three hours. But it was very hard to do this with my schedule. Then at night I would go to the gym. I would hit it haaaarrd! I would only be at the gym for about ninety minutes. I started a new program I created for myself. I loved it!

This workout consisted of a cardio session followed by time throwing the weights around. I would do twenty minutes of HIIT training with the running workout. Next, I lifted four exercises per body part, doing a different body part each day. I would hit them hard and fast. This way I would burn calories as I lifted. I did both upper and lower abs, but on an incline to give added intensity to it.

I did some research on why I was not seeing my abs on bodybuilding. com and found I had stubborn, hard to get rid of body fat covering them. The professionals suggested I circuit my abs. A circuit is when you keep a fast tempo when you workout. You are not taking rests in between sets. When I tried this, I was still breathing heavy from the HIIT all the way through the workout. And, I started seeing results. I started seeing my abs almost instantly. Finally, it was coming together.

My mind and grades were also transforming, thank God. Finally! I was passing all my classes with B's for the first time since high school. Papers returned would have grades like 92 or 89 on them. I couldn't believe my eyes. Every paper I turned in with confidence. Two reasons why this was happening to me. One, God had his hands on me, and he was going to make sure I was okay in everything. He would see to it that I succeed in everything I did right now. The second reason was that I had good work ethic. The day the paper was assigned I would start/finish it. Whenever I was bored I would go over my work. I already had my paper done and I would hear everyone else say, "Oh my God! I haven't even started that yet." And I would just think "Mine's done." If anything came up, I wouldn't have a conflict and I could go because I never had work to do.

There's always that one class you just can't do well in no matter how hard you try. Well, this for me was oceanography. I took this class thinking we would be learning about dolphins and sharks . . . ya' know? The ocean, it turns out, is all about fault lines and earthquakes. Not only was it boring and the teacher unexciting and monotone, but we had to take standardized tests. As you know, I don't do well in these types of classes . . . . so it was a struggle to get through.

I used to think drinking, for me, meant life or death. But now I didn't even think about it. God wasn't going to let anything happen to me as long as I was careful and not an idiot about it God had a plan for me. He wanted me to do great things. This doesn't mean I wasn't cautious when I drank, but I did not worry any more about what would happen the next day.

My friend Williana and I would play catch every Tuesday and Thursday after Political Science 101. I still had difficulty catching the ball at times. Still, I kept trying. I kept telling myself one day I would be out on that diamond playing ball. There were times I would play catch in my room and I would just stop and sit and stare in amazement at myself and what God had planned for me. I always told myself I would be famous, somehow, and I always told myself I would play Division 1 baseball if not go pro, no matter what everyone else thought. I was always too small, too skinny, not tall enough, but now it looked as though God may actually let me prove to everyone that I was going to do something great with my life. I didn't know what it was but something great would happen to me. I used to tell myself "if I go through hell now and end up being normal again, then it was all worth it."

At this point in my life I was beginning to actually be happy that the accident had happened to me. I know anyone reading this book right now is asking, "how can he say that after all that he has been through?" But, is that this accident made me a better person. I loved who I had become! Before the accident I conformed to what was "cool" in high school. I drank almost every night, went to school drunk, wanted to have the most beautiful girl in the school, and bragged to my friends about what girls I got with and what I'd done with them. Except I stuck to one rule that my father taught me; I would never take advantage of girl when they had been drinking. Now, I wanted a cute girl, with great personality. I never drank, I was always the DD so I could make sure my friends were safe and had rides.

During this spring semester, I went home for a long weekend and my parents wanted me to do some yard work. This way they could give me money because I was a broke college kid. I was planned to work for a couple hours each day. I worked for a couple on Saturday, then Sunday came. I had been badgering my father all day, "Let's go hit or play catch."

"No, I got to work," was the answer received. So, with my head down pouting, I grabbed my broom and headed outside to do some yard work, which lasted about a half-hour. I had to hit or something. It was way too nice a day to not play baseball. Although I should have been working, I grabbed my bat and a ball and walked up to the little league field.

Since I had no one to throw the ball to me, and I didn't have a tee, I figured throwing up the ball and hitting it would work on my hand-eye coordination. I did that for fifteen minutes then decided to watch the little leaguers in the field next to the cages play for a little bit.

"Man! I wish I could go back to those days, not a care in the world, just baseball." I watched those carefree kids laugh while they hit the ball, ran bases, and enjoyed this New England spring day. Then my dad pulled up to the curb.

Man, I was worried he was going to yank me into the car for leaving the yard work.

"What are you doing?" he asked me.

"Well, I was throwing the ball up and hitting it, but just stopped."

"Well, do you want me to throw to you?"

"I thought you had to work?"

"Na, I don't feel like working."

That was all he needed to say. He grabbed the bucket of balls that he always had stowed away in his car and brought it into the cage. I had been watching the Red Sox and my boy Dustin Pedroia. I analyzed his swing. How could it be that someone so small in stature could hit absolute bombs? Then I saw it, finally. He was a weight transfer hitter. I realized I could do something similar. So, in the cage I tried it out. My father was impressed with my bat speed. I had to work on making solid contact every time, but I was trying something new out and was hitting peas. I was ripping the cover off the ball. The only thing I didn't like about my new approach to hitting was on off-speed and slow pitches, I couldn't control my weight and my timing was way off. I ended way ahead of the ball. Then my dad found my weakness. Pitches that went low outside, I tried to pull it, and you are supposed to go with the ball. My dad, finding this, exploited my weakness. He wouldn't stop throwing there until I finally went the other way with the ball. Then, he wanted to see how I would do against faster pitching. Twenty feet away, he chucked the ball at me. I was hitting seeds. He would throw a curve ball in there and I couldn't touch it. Well, that's not true, I could hit his "lazy curve," which was a little more loopy than his "straight curve." His "straight curve" was fast and had a sharp break, but he kept throwing it to me until I got a good piece of one.

I said to him a few times that my hand hurt because I was beginning to get blisters. He said, "Zach, you're going to go back to school and take finals. You can let your hands heal then." Finally, the pain began to affect my swing. I looked at them and they were covered in blood, and had chunks of skin missing. All I said was, "Yeah, I think it's about time to stop." I laughed to myself. I actually missed this pain. I loved it! I'm back in it, able to work as I could until pain or an injury force me to take a break. But, we weren't done. No, we still had work to do. We got out the gloves to play catch.

I didn't have my glove and had to use my old one that was a 12'-inch, which made me nervous because the glove that I had been practicing with was a 13-inch. Which may not seem like a big difference, but when you don't know how close your arm will get to where the ball is, every inch counts. But my father threw the ball and my left hand went right to it. I caught every ball except, for balls on my left side. I was having a hard time with those. My dad threw fly balls and I was there every time. I had no problem tracking them. However, what my father was most impressed with was the strength of my right arm. I was reaching him effortlessly and directly on target. All in all, I did extremely well and was satisfied with what I had done on the day.

One thing did not change, however. Basketball I could not play it for the life of me. I could not catch a pass, dribble, or layup. I was terrible. How could it be that I could hit a fastball traveling at 95 mph, but couldn't run and dribble and bring the ball up to shoot? Too much coordination for my brain to handle, I figured. Also, it likely was that I didn't practice playing basketball like I did baseball. I didn't spend hours targeting specific moves and areas of my body.

At 5 a.m., the alarm sounded, and I had to get my ass to the gym. I was to meet Mike Todrin, the strength and conditioning coach for the UMass crew team. Mike was a cool guy and extremely nice and friendly. I had met him the day before in the gym. I was doing pull ups and while resting he approached me and asked if he could hop in and use the pull up bar. Then he does this crazy thing where he turns up-side down, hoisted his legs in the air and paused. "You're pretty talented, huh" I said when he finished. He started talking to me about how everything he does involves his core, then I pretty much finished his sentence when he said your core helps you with balance. Next, we got into an in-depth conversation on balance and coordination. He asked, "How do you know that much about balance and coordination?"

I told him I was in a car accident and had to do some physical therapy. Then he said, "That's how I got into doing abs and coordination, I was hit by a car on my bike." So I thought he could relate to my story. I told him about the car accident and how far I had come, how much I had learned in rehab and all the physical therapy sessions. Mike was awestruck. He couldn't believe what I had achieved.

Then, he gave me pointers on lifting and I gave him some more pointers on how to recover and where to get rehab, and we exchanged numbers. "You should totally do a workout with me," he said. I was all for it. I believed this was another one of God's movements in my life. "I workout at 5:30 am," he said. And me being the idiot I was responded with "Yeah! No problem. That will work out great for me. I always workout in the morning." Forgetting that I got little no sleep every night. My daily routine was getting to sleep at 330 a.m. and waking at 7:30 a.m. if I was lucky. Looks like I had to make a change.

All of his work-outs contained balance and coordination. In order to play baseball again, I had to switch all focus from my body to my brain. I had to get my mind right in order to play baseball at the Division One level. Mike said jokingly, "I've always wanted to work with a baseball player. I'll have you being the first .400 hitter since Teddy ball game." Or he would talk about the drills that he wanted to do with me if we had more time. "I'm going to get you like a Samari, you would balance on one leg and take cuts off the medicine ball."

I believed yet again this was God's work. I was just saying to myself the day after I hit with my dad, "Damn, I need to do more balance and coordination things. I need to completely change my workout". The next day I bump into Mike. Again, I sat in my room and just looked at my Jesus nailed to the cross figurine fixed to my wall and just said thank you God. "There won't be a day that I don't preach your name."

I emailed coach Stone and wanted to meet with him. This is what he wrote back:

Zach;

We are playing a lot of games, travelling, etc. at this point, so it's tough to give you an exact time . . . . Why don't you stop by the office on your way to the weight room sometime next week. We can talk for awhile and come up with a plan for the future.

Coach Stone

Everything was going my way! For once in my life after the accident, everything I wanted was happening. People would walk by me and Jon and just stare because I was having so much fun and laughing at myself. I was waiting for something to go wrong because every time since the accident, when I thought my life was getting better, I would come crashing down.

To make sure I would be able to play, I did everything I could. I don't just mean in the gym, but everywhere I went. In public, private, or even the omelet line at school. Yes, I was the weird kid in the front of the omelet line that everyone could see standing on one foot and hopping around. I would move my hands in a kung-fu motion to practice keeping my balance while using my upper body. I didn't care what anyone thought of me or my public actions, I was going to play baseball again. I told myself, "Right now everyone laughs at me because they do not know why I am doing this. But when they see me on ESPN one day, they will understand."

I paid a visit to coach Stone when we all returned to school. Not much was said, but that wasn't the point of the meeting. I set the meeting up because I wanted him to see me one last time before summer, to see what progress I had made over the past year. I believed it worked. Other than being impressed with my workout, he did not say anything or give me any obvious body language that said "Wow Zach, you look good." But the whole meeting I could tell by the way he looked at me and asked questions that he was amazed at how good I looked and what I had achieved. I talked about God and how I felt he was looking out for me and he wanted me to do this. Then I shook his hand and left. I felt good when I left the meeting, but still wondered what this meant to my future.

I had just returned from one of my classes and plopped myself on my futon. I placed my laptop on my lap and decided to check my away message to see what kind of IM's I had gotten. I was horrified at what I read. Bobby Kincaid was a kid in high school, who had gotten into a car accident. He ended up like I had, well, actually worse than I had.

My mom wrote me an IM, like she usually did to tell me how proud she was of me and it read: "On Saturday dad and I drove past Bobby Kincaid's house and saw him sitting outside in a wheelchair. I said to Dad that you were so blessed. I just read the paper and Booby died Sunday afternoon from complications from his accident. He was just starting to improve, it said in the paper. This could have been you and your life and for some reason God said "Not zach." Think of every breathe that you take as a blessing. I know we do. Love you, have a good day."

I replied, "ooo mom thats deep . . . I didn't even know him and I feel terrible"

I felt absolutely horrible. To think that could have been me. His life after his accident was one of no mobility. He was confined to a wheelchair, had communication problems, and had no one but his mother who had to quit her job to take care of him. The only one who paid any attention to him. I felt terrible because here I was depressed over baseball or a girl.

At least I could be depressed over these things. Bobby could not. He was never able, after the car accident, to experience the comfort of the love of a women or the enjoyment of playing baseball. At least I got a taste.

My away message after was: "R.I.P. Bobby . . . . you will live through my actions and achievements . . . . no one knows what life was like for us . . . . just because I was luckier than you doesn't mean u will b forgotten . . ."

I am truly blessed and GOD has a plan for me. Thank you GOD!

CHAPTER 9

WORKING HARD

When I thought of the upcoming summer, I feared it was not exactly going to be fun. There would be a lot of hard work that would hopefully get me that much closer to accomplishing my goal. First I had to finish my final exams. When I had to take my oceanography makeup exam for being sick and missing the first one, the only other kid taking a makeup exam in oceanography happened to have exam two, which is what I had. He was extremely smart and helped me on the group section. Because of his knowledge I ended up passing the test. Jon didn't get so lucky. I didn't do very well on the other course tests. In my Chinese myth and legends class, I had an A going into the final exam, didn't know a thing on the exam and failed it.

Now that school was pretty much over, with only a week remaining, Dianne wanted to set me up with her cousin, Lesly. We've already established that Dianne liked Jon even though she led me to believe I was who she was interested in. She hoped that maybe the four of us could double date. Yet again, I was getting far ahead of myself, planning out the future and whatnot. My injury made me do this continuously and it caused me a lot of stress.

The best thing about this whole situation was that I could not get hurt. For once in my life I was not invested in this girl . . . . IT WAS AWESOM E. The only thing I cared about was baseball and training. I had one goal in my life. Until then all other distractions must wait unless they fell in my lap and didn't give me any shit. Then, I was down to try them out. It was about time I finally learned how to deal with girls. Damn!

The Thursday before my brother Mike's graduation party, a couple of my Latin friends and I went to the bar, Lietrims, in Worcester. I was the designated driver as usual. We met up with Annie and all of her/ my friends. We were at the bar, once dancing got old, I couldn't help but stare at the television. Instead of having a beer or trying to get girl's numbers, I sat at the bar by myself, watching the Red Sox in Two (a replay of a game played that day). This is how much I loved baseball. Instead of trying to get laid or drinking to have a good time, I would rather watch baseball.

The night of my brother's graduation party, Dianne was supposed to bring her cousin for me to meet. I was not disappointed. Lesly was a very pretty Latina. She was a lot of fun, too. Everything was working perfectly, just how I wanted it. Dianne and Lesly were best friends/ cousins and Jon and I were best friends/ brothers. Lesly and I started to talk more and more, starting to share fun stories, and I started to relax. Everything I wanted was happening. I could just relax. This was exactly like freshman year all over again, except Lesly was Toni. See, when I have a girl that I know won't give me any problems and I know wants to be with me, I can just relax. I didn't have to worry about anything. So I began to have visions of Lesly being my girl. I would be able to relax and focus on baseball, maybe even hit that .750 I did on JV when I was a freshman in high school. But I wasn't going to let a girl get between me and my dreams. This was once again a premature thought.

You readers can see how one day I would think I'm in love with one girl then the next it would be another. My brain was so messed up . . . it's not funny, it's true. I was so confused and perplexed on how I could be in love with one girl then overnight wake and be in love with another. I went so far as to say to myself the next girl I date will be the one I marry because I can't do this anymore. This caused even more stress.

Then, as the semester came to a close, I started to not work as hard for baseball. Maybe the daunting idea of summer with no promise of reward drained me. I grew content with not working as hard. At first I thought it was just my body telling I knew there was something out there for me to accomplish and I just had to find it. I COULD DO THIS! But, I had to keep working as hard as I had before because that is what has gotten me this far . . . so I had to just keep pushing myself, I couldn't give up now I just couldn't. So not working hard, was only a brief period that lasted maybe a week or so.

Every time I played catch it was like a puzzle I had to figure out. Every throw and every time I caught the ball I had to focus and concentrate on what I was doing and what was wrong with it. One day I would play catch flawlessly with only a couple dropped balls here and there. The next day I would be someone completely different. If I was tired or just lazy, I wouldn't move my glove to catch the ball. I would throw balls everywhere making Jon/ my dad run.

Jon would yell, "Concentrate! Don't get lazy" But some days I just couldn't. Still, Jon would make me play catch every day. It was great having him stay at my house.

Sprints became extremely hard for me as well. First, when I ran sprints I had to concentrate on bringing my knee straight, in the direction I was running so my left foot would not hook around my right leg and trip me. The next thing I had to concentrate on was my left arm. I had to focus on keeping my elbows out with open fists to stop hitting my shirt with my fists causing me to get disoriented. Third, I had to make sure my stride was correct. I ran well if I got my left leg extended in front of me. So I had to stay focused on my left, bringing it up and out. This was tedious but, I knew it would, like everything else, pay off in the end.

Through the summer I would wake early in the morning and run sprints. Jon and I slept in the same bed until we were able to get another one. Jon would tell me to wake him when I woke so he could run with me. But at the start of summer he began drinking way too much to wake early with me. He didn't have the energy to get out of bed and train. He finally realized these nights of hardcore drinking were taking a toll on his body. He told me his vision was starting to fade and he thought alcohol played a part in this.

We sat down and had a serious conversation. Right when I came into the cellar from the pool area he said, "I'm done. I'm not going to any more parties, I'm done." I was overjoyed to hear him say this because the night before he was an absolute idiot. I was trying to get him to leave the party and he wouldn't. He was being arrogant and acting like he didn't have to listen to me. But, he was also my brother, and family had to stick together. I had to help him out. When he told me he was done drinking and partying, I told him that I was done partying too.

It was time to stop partying and start getting serious about training. My friends weren't going to understand why I didn't want to see them, but I had too many reasons not to go out. One being to get Jon healthy again, two would be so we could train with sufficient rest because staying out until 4:30 in the morning then sleeping all day was no way for athletes to live.

So I made a vow to myself that I would not go out any more (unless it was the party of the year). I would do something baseball-related each night, such as run sprints at 9 o'clock. I would go to the gym twice a day, I would do core and balance exercises on one session and my lifts during the other session. I would do some type of cardio both sessions. I made sure it was at an HI level. I believed the HI running was/ is the best thing to help my brain heal.

Hitting with Jon not only kept me grounded, but made me strive to be even better. I would hit and make good contact, then I would throw to Jon and he would hit absolute bombs. It didn't bother me too much because he's a Division One football player, he can bench 350 something, and he should be able to hit the ball further than me. Yet, hitting with Jon also made me strive to be better. He was Division One football player, not a baseball player. I found myself afraid to be what I considered an everyday normal person I wanted to do something amazing. I felt there was something better out there for me to accomplish, something extraordinary. Ever since I was little I thought God had something planned for me.

I began to question my hitting stance. I could not find a stance that was comfortable, and I would start to worry I'd never be able to generate enough power. So for answers I looked to the greatest hitter who ever lived, Ted Williams. I began searching Youtube and other internet sites for more information about his perspective on hitting.

One area where all the hard work I put in improved my life was it made me a really good dancer. The running and training made my motor skills work properly and my coordination great. Finally, I could dance in public without being embarrassed. It was great! I danced everywhere, whenever I had a chance. I abused my privilege to dance because no one knew what it was like to not be able to move correctly, or attempt to dance and lose your balance. Now that I could dance I would dance as much as I could and wherever I could!

I decided to go bowling with my friends in Gardner. We tried to get some girls to come with us but they were all busy. So, we decided on a guy's night out. I didn't even put cologne on, didn't bother dressing up and wore a hat instead of gelling my hair. When we got to the bowling alley, I had one mindset; to bowl (I was in the zone, too). I was bowling an incredible game. I led all the way until the last frame of the match. I kept making a fool out of myself by dancing after every time I would bowl and made these girls in the lane next to me laugh.

I threw one ball down the alley after my signature dance. It was heading straight down the alley on target. I turned toward my friends with arms in the air like I was God of the bowling alley. I thought I had a strike. They all laughed at me. I turned and I had knocked all the pins down but one. The girls in the next lane laughed at me too. So I started talking to them, throwing in a couple one liners here and there.

One of the girls was quite cute. Around 5'4", blonde hair, the cutest brown eyes, and she had a cute body. So after I gave the girls high fives I came back to Derek, Travis, and Thomas. They were sitting and I asked them what they thought about the blonde one. They all said she was cute. I spit game to her all night. I asked Derek if she was cute enough to get her number and he of course said yes. So I got it. But then Travis said, "Invite her back to your house and have a quick hot tub sesh". I did and she jumped on the opportunity, and she texted me right after she left the bowling alley. All my friends could not believe I had that much game, to pick up a girl at a bowling alley.

Her name was Katie. Katie had colon cancer at a very young age. She went through a lot like I had. We related to each other and I believe this is the main reason we had such a connection. I could finally relate to a female with a similar background of overcoming tragedy. There weren't many people that I could relate to on this level. When all one wants is to fit in and one finally thinks what you are looking for is found, it's like you go blind to all other things.

She cared about me so much. Katie was such a sweet girl. She cared deeply for her friends and family, and this was a big attraction for me. I'll give you an example of how nice she was to all her friends. Just to see her best friend who lived forty minutes away, she would drive to get her then drive back home so they could hang out. She always offered to pay for me on the times I wasn't working.

Katie wasn't the hottest girl when I had first met her, but I didn't care. She was beautiful in my eyes. A beautiful person inside and that's all that mattered to me. She had a cute face, and I love a cute face! Katie definitely had potential. The face was there.

That was the biggest issue. She was only 17! It scared me that I was starting to like a 17 year-old and I was 20. So I told her we should just be friends, but we shouldn't stop dating. I was beginning to think that Katie and I were meant for each other. She had been through something as horrible as I, she needed someone to treat her well, and she actually cared about me.

I also started to think that we were destined for each other because I deserved a really good girl, and she deserved the world. I felt like I may be the guy to give her it. Where I thought I was heading with my life I could give her everything she wanted. If my plan came true I would be a professional baseball player with a story that would offer many endorsement deals. And if I never reached this goal, I hoped to be famous somehow, to speak about God, and how he has helped me cope, helped recover from the accident or maybe just help people with brain injuries. Only time will tell.

As the summer continued, Katie became very clingy and wouldn't give me any space. She began to text me all the time, show up at my house uninvited. So I knew I had to ABORT! Her parents were also starting to freak me out. They would send Facebook messages and things they would say to me for example the mother inboxed me on Facebook one day and wrote a nasty message that said Katie was sad and that "I don't know what happened but it didn't happen with me!" I feared I got in way too deep, way too fast. So I told her let's just be friends and not date. I had way too much stuff on my plate. I didn't need a girlfriend or anything that resembled one. I felt really bad, but it was summer and that meant, for me, hard work.

After all this frustration, I got in my car and drove to Dicks Sporting Goods. I bought a tee that was "for" tee ballers. I didn't need anyone else. I would hit into the cage for hours. This way I would only need one ball, and I would never have to worry if my dad took the buckets with him to work. I drove instantly to the field to give it some use.

I took a tip from the great Ted Williams. It is bat speed, not bat weight, that matters, and I dropped from a 33-inch to a 32-inch. As I hit for an hour and a half, I placed the tee down the middle, inside, and outside. I changed where I would stand to hit the ball. For example, I would hit the ball further out in front of the plate if I placed the ball on the inside part of the plate, and if it was outside I would let the ball get a little more on top of me to hit it the other way. I noticed that I kept hitting ground balls not line drives. Only one thing could be leading to my ground balls;

my stance. Yes, that's right. The stance that I thought I had fixed was still giving me problems . . . again.

I tried to figure out what was giving me problems. Maybe I was striding too far and I'm getting on top of the ball. So, I tried different stances to find which one was best. I tried to shorten my stance so that maybe I would stop over-striding, but still more groundballs. Maybe I should just do away with the step just like Sid and I had done a couple years ago. Maybe it was too much to worry about stepping and then worrying about hitting a baseball. So I lifted up my heel (but stayed on the balls of my feet) with my feet shoulder length apart and putting it down when I was about to hit. I hit 3 line drives in a row right up the middle. I thought I had found it. But, I had felt this way before.

I used to lie to my parents and tell them I was going to the mall or a friend's house. When in reality I would drive to the little league field to take hacks. My parents had an idea of what I was doing. My mom would say, "I think you should play softball next summer. I think that you would be good at it." After my mom would say these things I would sit and think to myself, as I watched MLB network, "One day, it may not be this fall when I try out, but one day." I hoped it would be this fall so I would quit having to wait and I could finally play baseball.

Some days I would wake at 8ish and mentally prepare myself to go to the gym. If I wasn't focused on going to the gym and making gains, then it would be a bad gym day. I would go to the gym and do my HI running for a half hour. On the way home I would stop at the little league field, put together my tee, and take the one ball I had and hit for another half hour. A half hour was sufficient because I still had another gym session in the afternoon, when I went with off Jon Hernandez (Jhern) and Jon Rodriquez (Jrod) at the gym.

This became my routine every day. My physical therapist told me it was best to work when I was tired. I did this routine for a little while, but I was sick of looking in the mirror and seeing what I considered to be a fat body. I only had a little fat on my belly, but to me I was obese. I was sick of it. I went balls to the wall and never looked back for a month. I started going to the gym three times a day.

I would wake up at 8, go to the gym and do my running HIIT workout. After, I did exercises that helped my core and coordination. Next, I went home and ate. I would rest for a couple of hours then I would bring Jrod and Jhern to the gym. We went to the high school gym instead of my gym because they did not have a membership. Posted up on a wall was a baseball workout for the high school team. I knew it was a legit workout because I knew the coaches that made it, and they knew what they were talking about. They played for Brown University and St. Josephs University. I decided to do this work out to gain strength, and on days that I was not supposed to lift I would just focus on core and getting those abs.

I would go to my gym at night and focus on cardio. I did the stair-master for a half an hour, then to the row machine and row 2,000 meters at 30 strokes per minute. I then followed this up by doing core and focusing on my abs.

I was working so hard that there wasn't a day I wasn't completely exhausted by the end I stopped calling my friends, and I had told Lesly and Katie that I was too busy to hangout. But, if you want something, "go get it" right? I was absolutely determined that I would play for UMass. Not only would I make the team, but I would start in left field and if I didn't bat .400 or close to it, then the season would be a disappointment. If I kept setting goals for myself to reach then I could never grow content with what I had achieved thus far. Until I reach perfection, I have not accomplished anything.

Being a perfectionist is what kept me working hard. But I am only a perfectionist when it comes to two things; baseball and my body. That's why I was so depressed when I could not achieve a perfect body no matter how hard I worked. Everything else I didn't give a shit about. If you told me to do a math problem such as 2+2 and I would win a great prize, I would say 3 just so I could go hit off a tee.

I began getting forearms with protruding veins, they looked jacked. Also my back was getting bigger and more cut. I could only think that God was helping me out. Again, I thought that he wanted me to do this; wanted me to achieve greatness.

After all the hard work I put in to get back to baseball, I thought that I should try to enjoy myself a little. Even though, everything was coming together, from baseball to my body, I still felt as though I was missing something. Yes, a girl. I couldn't fight it. I just wanted someone to cuddle with, a companion. Jon was getting back with his ex, Kaylin. I felt it was time for me to work for the girl of my dreams. Dianne. I realized that as great as Katie was, deep inside the real reason I could not get with Katie was because of Dianne. I liked her so much, that I had to have her.

CHAPTER 10

REALIZATION

After a week of hard work I decided that I should go to this party Dianne's brother was throwing. Dianne's brother was a friend since sophomore year in high school. He was a great guy and he invited 'The Spain Train', which contained Jhern, Puky, Jrod, me, my asian friend Outahi and Sam Garcia, but he wasn't present. I knew Dianne would be there so I planned out what I was going to say. She looked so cute, even though she was wearing little to no make-up.

There she was. "So adorable," I thought to myself. "She looked absolutely beautiful." I said hello to her first, to be nice. To feel it out. Later, when I bent down to pet the dog running around me she came up to me. After joking and laughing with her the whole night, I pulled her aside. I decided to put everything on the line, tell her exactly how I feel. That way she'll know." This is exactly what I did.

I started off with "Dianne, I like you. A lot." Then she brought up her cousin, Lesly. I told her that I did not like Lesly. That I had liked her, and that I now only liked her as a friend. I said I would do anything for Dianne, that she was my dream girl. "I just wanted to tell you how I feel, and that all I wanted was her friendship and to see her more often."

Then, we did our own thing the rest of the night. I felt things went well. Most of all, it felt good to get things off my chest and finally tell Dianne exactly what was in my mind and heart. Now I would wait for Dianne to decide what she wanted.

Too bad it back fired. I couldn't get Dianne off my mind, I would constantly think about her. She didn't even like me back, she didn't return my texts, she didn't call, I got no interaction yet I still could not get her off my mind. My training for baseball began to suffer. Instead of concentrating on the task at hand I thought only of Dianne. To the point that I almost gave up on baseball.

After a day of terrible training, I relaxed in bed and reflected on my life. I thought about how sad my life really was. It did not help that the day before I found a book Natasha made for me with all the newspaper clippings from my accident, and letters all this junk about how she loved me "always and forever." I began to think about how though I worked so hard I seemed to get nowhere. I was fed up. Why bother. No matter what I do I don't get anywhere. I can live a happy life without baseball and I could, instead of working toward baseball, focus my attention on getting the girl of my dreams.

I didn't want to go to the gym, but I made myself go anyway. I still wanted a nice body. I only did twenty minutes on the stair master and went to do some abs. In the middle of an ab routine, I got pissed that I would just give up on myself like that, yet again. I said to myself, "You're a pussy, I'm just going to give up on myself like that? If I worked this hard and only got this far this meant I needed to work even harder." So I got in my car and drove away to the baseball field to hit off of the tee.

One day, when it was raining, I went to the field and I began throwing the ball and catching it to practice pop-flys. My depth perception was terrible from remaining some double vision when a small target would move fast. I started the exercise and I was an absolute fail. The ball would land in my glove, but my hand would jerk or flail and I dropped the ball. When I threw the ball high in the air I couldn't track it. I tried to get underneath the ball, but I just couldn't. I would lose sight of it. This was a lot different than before the accident where I would effortlessly track a fly ball. I kept telling myself to concentrate, repeated it every throw, and only then did I start to catch some fly balls. I started to think that maybe I should concentrate on things I could already do rather than hoping if I work hard enough I will be able to do certain things. I accepted the fact that I could see ground balls clearly; fly balls not so much.

Of course, the inability to catch fly-balls would limit positions where I'd be effective. I began playing around with the idea of playing an infield position. This would be hard because I had always been afraid of the ball because when I was little, I was playing shortstop and a groundball shot at me like a missle and bounced up and hit me directly in the throat. So balls on the ground coming at me, always scared me. But after everything that I went through, a leather ball with some stitches in it wasn't going to keep me from playing baseball again. "If this is what I have to do", I thought to myself, "then this is what I will do. It may be uncomfortable at first but I will do it." Yet, in a way, this transition would be a lot easier than learning how to catch fly balls again. When I look up I see two baseballs, but when I look down or straight out it is pretty much one. Playing infield, my depth perception or lack thereof would not be as much of a factor.

I started out early in my life very good playing infield until one day I was playing short stop in little league. I went to dig out a ground ball and it took a bad hop and got me right in the throat. I rolled on the ground and gasped for air, but I couldn't get any. My throat swelled shut. It was one of the scariest moments of my life. Also, when s in high school I was the fifth infielder for tight situations. I frequently made incredible diving plays when the was hit right at me. I slyly got out of the way and fielded it to the side of my body.

As the summer progressed, I debated what position I should tryout for. I was afraid pitching might be the only way for me to tryout. It would be the only way for me not to use my weaker, less coordinated left side. I asked my dad if he would work with me on throwing a knuckleball. I was not going to hit 92 on a gun, so if I had a knuckleball it didn't really matter how hard I threw.

I was confused, but if I wanted to try out for the team at UMass, I had to keep all my options open.

The night before I went to the field to pitch with my dad and brother, I stayed up all night and watched YouTube videos on throwing certain pitches. I was determined God wanted me to pitch. I thought this because my right side could dominate and I would not need my left side as much. It would take all that I had to get to Division 1 form, but I could do it. July 4th, I went to the field with my dad and brother. My dad and I took turns throwing several buckets, to my brother. I saw that this was going to be a very long process, but I could work on all the things that I needed for pitching by myself. I did not have to rely on anyone else to work on balance and release points. I had far to go because in order to begin to practice my knuckleball I had to get my form correct on my fastball; that was going to take awhile.

Every day between workouts, I would throw a ball off the wall of my garage. Sweat would drip down my face and cover my body. This was good practice on my form for groundballs. Because of my new found obsession with groundballs and training all day, every day, for baseball, my mom began to worry again. She asked me what my plans were for baseball. I couldn't tell her until I had conquered my skills. I did not want to tell her because she would worry about my well-being. Because I wasn't telling her and talking to her about it, she started to find alternatives to baseball. "Hey, honey, you should try softball. The ball is bigger and it goes really slow. So I think you'll be a good hitter." I loved my mom always trying to make my life better, easier. I replied, "I don't want to." Then she would ask five times "Why?" I repeated over and over, "I don't want to . . . I don't want to." I could not tell her the real reason was that I was spending hours upon hours training for baseball tryouts.

I wasn't afraid of playing softball. I wasn't afraid of death so softball sure wasn't going to put fear in me. I wish I could explain to you why I felt this way about death. The best way I can explain is I just don't think death is a big deal. When I used to drive on the highway with my friends, I would tend to drift of the side of the road near the guardrail. My friends would always freak out. To me it was no big deal, I was in control. I knew we weren't going to hit the guard rail, so I just shook it off. I just didn't find things of alarming. As long as I was in control, I knew I would be safe. It almost felt like I had no reason for concern because I had been through the worst, this was no big deal.

After going through everything I've gone through, and having the whole world look down on me not believing that I could bounce back, nothing can scare me from accomplishing my goals. Especially not groundballs! I truly did fear them, but I would conquer them like I conquered walking, swallowing, talking, running; all the activities they said I would never be able to do.

Many days my routine became; wake up at 8:00 a.m.; go to the gym and do cardio, abs, and forearms; stair master for a half an hour either on a HI or do a HIIT workout. I would be drenched in sweat. When my mom and dad went to the gym the same time as me, they yelled at me and told me I needed to bring another shirt. After I left the gym I would drive to the field and hit off the tee by myself for a half hour. I would go home, cook up some eggs, then help my dad or my parents with whatever they needed done around the house. This was basically my daily summer routine.

When I finally told my dad about trying out for the team, the conversation went like this:

Dad- "the coach won't waste a spot or his time on a junior."
Me- "Coach Stone wants me to try out."
Dad- "Zach, you are nowhere near the old Zach."
Me- "I'm going to work my ass off to get there"
Dad- "I will work with you to get your skills back but just don't get your hopes up that you'll make the team."
Me- "I don't expect to but I want to at least try out, I think this may be God's plan for me."

Dad nods his head and says "I'll help you but don't expect to make the team."

Yet I still had no doubts that I would make the team.

I found another issue I had to overcome. My concentration was terrible when people watched. I would have perfect form and perfect timing, feeling confident, then someone would unexpectedly start watching and I couldn't do anything. I lost focus and concentration. My brain spun the questions, "Are they watching? Hey, look what I can do. Look where I've arrived. I hope they saw that one." I wouldn't concentrate on the task at hand. Concentration is one of the most difficult elements to get back after a brain injury, which is why I am surprise I was able to do well in college and pass.

My doctor told me that concentration is difficult when you receive a TBI because you injure multiple levels. It is different than when you injure another part of your body. When you injure your brain, depending on where the injury happens you are injuring control of consciousness, memory, cognition, concentration, balance, vision among other things. When you injure a muscle you are only inhibiting that muscle and its function. It takes longer to heal the brain. You must overload it to heal it. This means you must put excess strain on your mind to get it to heal.

And then it happened again. The negative self-talk. "Move on Zach, you are training too hard for something you don't even know you can achieve. No girl wants to date you because you won't let them get close enough. You are so obsessed. Just give up Zach. Find a job and get a girl."

But I told myself I would work as hard as I could until junior year tryouts. If I didn't make it I could move on.

Joe developed a training facility 'The Ultimate Athlete' complete with a hitting cage and Astroturf. The first time I went there I hit off the tee for a very long time. Then I moved to the pitching machine. Bad idea! I didn't make contact with one ball. It was absolutely terrible.

I could not figure out hitting! My lower body was set, my hips, my stance, everything was all good. But I could not figure out where to put my hands.

When I was at the gym with Jrod I kept trying to get my hands right. My back elbow was falling below my wrists, which for me wasn't good. I needed to have my back elbow cocked and ready to explode. When I cocked my back elbow I would hit shots off the tee and straight line drives.

Back at the field with this new stance, which was basically my old stance, I hit brilliantly. I couldn't get excited though because I had felt this way before. That night I went to Joe's place again and he threw me around 100 balls. At first I was swinging way too hard. I was making contact but getting lazy groundballs. I got tired of swinging hard, loosened my swing, and drove the ball straight to the back of the cage. How could this be? If I wasn't swinging hard then how could I be driving the ball so hard? Maybe all I had to have was a good lower stance, comfortable hands, and God would do the rest. It was almost like my hands were just going through the motions, but making solid contact every time.

I had to get a grip on reality and stop living in this fantasy world where all my dreams could come true. I had great opportunities to get involved at the gym and start my career, but I was too stubborn to stop trying to play baseball.

And I realized it was like I had an addiction to girls like an addiction to a drug. I was addicted to the company of a girl. I felt it was necessary to have to could continue with life, be happy, and be successful. I cannot explain how big a burden this was. I was psychologically confused. So much so, I went through a Taco Bell drive through to get the number of a girl who worked there. She was of course, Latina.

Then I met this cute little Asian girl, Sophia, at a party. She had been in my French class in high school freshman year. Yet, I had no idea who she was but she knew me. She immediately caught my eye. She was very pretty, and pretty short, 5'1", and I love short girls! I was playing beer pong and I yelled to Sophia to come talk. I made her laugh, and her friend came over and we started talking. Then I got her friend's number, not Sophia's.

The next day I went on Facebook and wrote a message to Sophia asking for her number. She gave it to me so I texted her that same day. I asked her out to ice cream and she said yes. This was my first real date since I had dated Katie. So I got there and of course she didn't get an ice cream, but my fat ass had to have one. We talked and we joked. I do not know what came over me, but I had this surge of confidence. I asked her to go back to my house to watch a movie and maybe go swimming.

As soon as we got back home I put on a movie and she was all over me. Not like making-out, but she was holding my arm and getting very close to me. This was an unbelievable feeling. With Natasha this never happened. I never felt good enough for Natasha. Sophia and I had a lot of fun at my house. We hung out and watched a movie with me kissing her on the forehead or the cheek. At the end of the night we made plans to hangout the next day. I wondered if by me telling God that I was going insane without a girl and that I needed one, he answered in the form of Sophia.

I had great friends, I could choose at any moment to be a personal trainer, Sophia and I had a good thing started, and I was all set. Considering I was alive, why did I need anything else? I remember when I was with Sophia telling myself *Maybe you need to have sex with a girl for them to stay with you. That's what everyone else does.* Well I was wrong because the day after we had sex she told me that she had just gotten out of a four-year relationship Within two weeks she said it was too soon to jump into another one. And besides, I would be leaving for school in a week. You can imagine how confused this made me but I just wrote it off at another failed attempt to make this new life I had make sense.

I learned through experience with Sophia some important things. I did have to learn how to become a man all over again! What I mean by this is that, I had to learn to stop letting things bother me and just go with the flow. I stopped caring so much. Just like a man, I was beginning to see how people have things to do and they need to do what they have to do. Other people don't have concern for me, I am the only one who is concerned about me.

All I wanted to do at this point in my life was move on from baseball. It was time to stop living in a dream world. My mother was right. I felt as though God made me want to play baseball these past years to motivate me so that I would work as hard as I could. Before it was baseball, baseball, baseball. Now it was my body, a career, creating a job, and getting a girl. I was so sick of living in a state of limbo Getting a job was always a struggle for me because if I made the baseball team, I'd have to make the team a priority. Not anymore. I was sick of not knowing what my future held when the key was in my hand. I control my own destiny! All I wanted to do was become a personal trainer or work in a gym I seriously began to ponder whether or not I should even tryout for the team. I began to stress. Tryouts were only a week away!

I thought baseball was my obsession when in reality I was always obsessed with my body and the way it looked. I loved going to the gym for hours, although I did love to go hitting and it was a stress reliever. But the gym gives an instant sense of accomplishment; you work as hard as you can and you get results from your hard work. Only you could make a difference in what your body looked like. It was all you. You didn't have to worry about other people in the gym like you had to worry about other players on the field in baseball, or worrying where the coach thought you belonged. Just you, the dumbbells, and a mirror.

I really just didn't care anymore what people would think if I walked away from baseball. All I wanted was that flat stomach and big biceps. I felt practically like a normal human again. People laugh when I say this, but it's true. No one knows what it was like for me with the inability to dance at a party because I did not have coordination, and without balance I was afraid I would fall. But without the stress of playing baseball I was free. During this time I wanted to be a personal trainer and tell my story to the world.

I emailed Coach Stone and told him I had to sort out some personal issues and that I wanted to try out for baseball next year, although I'd be senior. He replied with this:

Zach,

I understand and hope that everything is OK and that you are making progress and will be able to tryout next year.
Good luck this year.

Coach Stone

Mike Stone
Head Baseball Coach
UMass/Amherst

Now I could try out for the team if I wanted to, even as a senior. When school started I was not thinking about baseball. I could finally concentrate on my grades and my body and get them both right.

CHAPTER 11

STRAIGHTENING OUT MY LIFE

J unior year of college already. It seems like just yesterday I was lying in a hospital bed unable to walk. It was time to stop wishing that I was on the baseball diamond. It was time to completely transform my body. That meant it was time to start my nutrition plan.

My nutrition plan contained nothing but proteins and vegetables. I think the absolute hardest thing to do was to give up eating late night or eating bad foods (carbs) at night. It was so tempting because Jon and I would go late night and hangout with Cozzo and the rest of the football team. They always served something absolutely delicious, but also always the worst thing one could eat for my nutritional goals.

A couple of days went by when I realized something. Tryouts for this year's baseball team went by and I didn't even think about them nor my not playing. I didn't even miss it. It was great! Even though deep inside I still had a burning desire to play, I could now move comfortably on with my life. That was the first step.

Now to figure out this whole girl situation. Looking back, I should of stopped stressing about girls a lot sooner than I did.

Although I felt good about myself getting over baseball, something was definitely going on with my brain. I told myself it was my brain in its last healing process, the swelling subsiding indefinitely, but this was only my belief. But boy did it hurt. I would get severe headaches every day. They were similar to the ones I would get before the accident, but I never got them every day like this. And I was having memory problems. I couldn't remember anyone's name. Five seconds after someone would tell me their name I would have to ask them what their name was again. I just hoped that this was the final stage in my healing process, that I would actually soon be a normal person. I didn't go to a doctor or see any one because I thought the headaches just came with the territory of having a brain injury.

But, nevertheless I was still going to the gym and doing a lot of cardio. I was also still following my nutrition plan and saw great result. Only a week and I started to see my abs more and more each day. I was extremely happy. This is all I had to do this whole time! Just cut out sugars and almost instantly look better! But with the sugars, I also monitored carb intake. I got it down to around 20 grams a day. It was definitely tough but definitely worth it in the end.

I was consumed with my body and amazed at how my nutritional program and workout routines were working, but then I went to the UMass football game v.s. Albany. We beat them 44-7. Jon played a lot as the back-up tail back. Our friend Adam came to visit and watch Jon play. He couldn't stop talking about how, "Finally someone out of Leominster is making something out of themselves." This made me wonder was I too going to make something out of myself or was I meant to be a coulda' been? I knew I didn't want to be a coulda' been so when I saw Jon run for a 50-yard touchdown, two emotions flooded me.

One was happiness, obviously. My brother for the last 2-3 years was doing big things and getting recognized. The second was a bittersweet mix of inspiration and doubt. Why couldn't I do something great with my life? Just because I came from Leominster did not mean I had to fall to the wayside like so many before me. My path may be different, but I was going to make a name for myself. I couldn't give up on baseball, not yet. I had one year left to tryout. I know I said this before, but now I was seeing fast results. History of athletes in Leominster is not impressive. It is a history of great talent washed away by drugs and alcohol. That's why Jon's story is so amazing. To grow up where he did in a housing project and having to deal with that kind of temptation is inspiring. The ability to keep his head on straight was simply amazing. Kids from Leominster always got bit by the drugs and alcohol bug. Heck, I did. I became an alcoholic at 16.

If I dwelled on how I had thrown my life away and could never play a college sport, do you think I'd be where I am today? Even though I had thought I had fully moved on from baseball, I could hear it calling my name. It was a presence in my life, not the complete focus of it, but it still called me to keep working toward my original goal. A voice in the distance. A voice that you hear vaguely at first, but as you follow, it gets louder and more profound.

The only focus I had was my body. I had no distractions in my life. No more girls to worry about, which by the way I was sure Dianne was trying to play head games with me. When I asked Jon about it he said "they all do." But, now I wasn't paying attention to her and I think she was actually beginning to like me more. I couldn't of cared less.

At this point all I wanted to do was try out for baseball and give it a good shot. Not be another kid trying out, but be good enough to make people say, "Damn, this kid had to learn how to walk. At age 17." The key was not to get cocky. My mentality was that of a true competitor, a true athlete: "Ya, I know that I am amazing, and yeah, I know I should be dead or vegging in a chair. But look at how far I came to take your spot on the roster." And that's not me being conceded, but confident. With this mentality no obstacle seems too far, or too out of reach. You could use this mentality for any avenue in life.

Baseball was an afterthought. I could now do everything normal. That included dancing, working out, and just being a young adult. Plus, my personality was back in full swing. I didn't have time to worry about baseball. I had so much going for me, I didn't know where to concentrate!

School was getting harder and harder, though. The more I attended class, the more I hated it. The respective professor would just go on and on about things that I had no interest in. Things I would never have to use in my life. For example, my math teacher, great teacher, great guy but am I really going to need to know linear equations for my future of personal training. The only class I didn't mind was my nutrition class. I was good at the topic and found I was quite interested. I didn't want to learn about political science. Why the hell would I want to learn about political science? I want to be a personal trainer not a politician. So, it was very hard for me to concentrate. But I needed that degree right? After all, I was the guy who was told I'd never walk, much less read, and even more unlikely be awarded a degree in undergraduate studies.

It seemed it was even harder to concentrate than it was immediately after the accident. Which didn't make sense. As time went on I should be getting better, not worse. The fact of the matter is that I felt like I had better places to be. Like in the gym or online looking up more tips on how to lose body fat. Simply put, school just didn't interest me.

So, I put my knowledge of my body to the test and I hit the gym hard. I was lifting four days a week, with a high intensity cardio every day. I would often walk the treadmill at the end of my workout. I noticed when I walked on a high intensity walking pace (4.0) I would develop a limp. I would be striding too far and my left leg was not quick enough to get off of the tread. Every time I encountered a bump in the road like this I reminded myself to stop and concentrate. Every step I made sure not to over stride and snap my left foot off of the treadmill to generate enough leg speed so my leg would stride forward. I couldn't believe that three almost four years after my brain was altered that I still had to train parts of my body to work correctly.

One night I was invited to a party where I also invited Dianne and her friends. Dianne and crew got lost when I gave them the directions. So I went to go find them. They were cold so I brought them back to their dorm instead of going all the way back to the party. Dianne and I weren't ready to end the night yet, so we took a drive to listen to some reggaeton! We were singing and dancing, it was the most fun I'd had in awhile. Then Dianne, while we were driving around talking about how she felt like she was having a hard time fitting into UMass because "I have all these guy friends at home, but here I don't have any here." Then she said "Could we be best friends?" Knowing that this probably meant that I would never get the opportunity to be her boyfriend, I replied "Of course". Instead of feeling sad or mad, I was overjoyed!

There was another girl in my poly sci class, the class I couldn't have given a rat's ass about so I found other distractions. She was in my class a year ago too, and I didn't have the balls to introduce myself. She was one of those girls who you just look at and say to yourself *Out of my league, no shot*. Her name was Allysa and her major was poly sci. She was from NJ and a Yankee and Jets fan. Of course, the weekend after I met her, the Jets played the Pats and won. I heard all about it on Monday, on what Moss needs to do, what Brady needs to do. But before all this sports smack, she asked for MY number. I couldn't believe it. This was way too good to be true. Dianne wants to be best friends, and this beautiful girl is interested in me. I was just waiting for something to go wrong. When it seems too good, it usually is.

In all my experiences in college with women, I began to see how powerful of an effect women have on men. It truly is amazing to see how they tame a man who used to believe himself wild and free. Another thing I began to realize is how much I believed I needed a woman. In some ways it doesn't make sense how much a man would do for a woman they really like.

I watched this constant cycle with my friends falling for girls. One second your friends are going out with you every weekend then when they get a girl or their girl comes to visit they drop everything and you are off their radar. But, you know what? We're men, we understand the power of being with a women. We know there is no greater feeling; there is no greater ecstasy. So, you don't get mad or hold grudges when one of your boys makes plans with you and they end up hanging out with their girl. No, instead men sit and think, "Damn, I wish I had somebody."

Some people try to substitute that loneliness or solitude with drugs, alcohol, or even work. In college I discovered how much I truly wanted a girl. I was not trying to get one. I was so into my body and worrying about getting a job, worrying about myself and future, that when I was with a girl I found attractive I almost ignored them. I was nice to them, but I wasn't worried about making conversation as I had been when I was trying to get a girl. Instead, I was chillin. I was laid back focusing on myself.

But I needed to give girls opportunities. I couldn't shut them out because I would never give them a chance to get to know me. With Allysa, I sat next to her in class and she initiated conversation with me. The next class she asked for my number. That's all I had to do. As my dad always told me, "Just give them a chance. Make them come to you." I never understood this until now. It actually worked.

As I began to figure out the direction I wanted to go in life, I noticed I could not watch baseball. I would get this urge to play that burned deep inside. Thoughts of my playing and striving for the big leagues haunted me whenever I watched a Red Sox game. I limited myself to watch baseball in small amounts so it could not consume me.

During this time in my junior year, it seemed that bad things didn't happen to me anymore. At least those weird things out of the ordinary ceased to happen now. Things like my clothes getting stolen out of the drier. Oddball events seemed to stop. Life finally looked like it was turning around from all perspectives. Even if something small happened to me, an inconvenience, I learned to laugh it off. My life was going to be great, some way.

So, Allysa . . . she had a boyfriend back home. She explained this was why she had been so hesitant to hang out with me. Apparently, I was too tempting or something. I knew things were too good, too potentially wonderful for us. All I did when she texted about her boy was laugh. The night Allysa revealed her little secret, I decided to stay in. I wasn't feeling good anyway, but it was a Friday night. I should be going out, right? Anyways, I was watching NESN Sports Desk and there was a cancer survivor who played football for BC, his name was Mark Herzlich. A truly inspiring story but yet again, just like Hamilton, he did not have to start all over again to get to where he wanted or needed to be to play at the Division One level. I could not seem to find one person who had a debilitating incident that took them back to square one in life and after went on to prepare themselves physically and mentally to achieve the same path they were on before.

Teddy Bruschi, the host, told him, "Be proud you are a survivor". This caught my attention. I began to think how I had just begun being proud that I too was a survivor. Just like Teddy, just like Mark, I survived something and went on to do great things after experiencing the ordeal.

I began to tell more people my story, to show them some of the writings I'd done after and during college. I was no longer scared about what others were going to think. To me, it was the only way I could think. The writing and journal entries and scenes began to form, and in doing this exercise I hoped that maybe someone someday would learn a valuable lesson. That maybe I could save someone's life, or to someone whose life had changed perhaps I could give them hope.

During this time that Allysa wanted to hang out with me, I met a girl name Tosca. This girl was absolutely beautiful and she looked like she was Latina But, just like with Allysa, I couldn't get the balls my sophomore year to talk to her. She went to late night at the dining common every night and I saw her at dinner a lot. I still wouldn't talk to her. Then one day I almost backed into her with my car. You're probably thinking, "Smooth Zach." But I thought to myself, perfect! All I had to do was apologize and make it into sound like our near collision was a huge deal. She knew my name and a little later in our communication I got her number. But, I was not going to get excited about this one either.

I felt I was getting my mojo or my swagger back. I was becoming the Zach of old. No girl intimidated me. Nobody seemed out of my league. I would walk up to any girl and start a conversation with them. I didn't care because I would probably never see that girl again if she thought I was weird or whatever. All my friends seemed to admire that I would walk up to any girl in the room and start talking. But I couldn't get a girl who wouldn't play games with me. It was absolutely ridiculous.

It just seemed like every girl just wanted to play games with me, almost like they would tease me. I figured out why it was so easy for them to cause stress in my life. All I did was sit in my room when I wasn't working and I would think about girls. And I was by myself a lot. Jon always had football and many of my other friends lived off campus. I concluded that I needed a job. That should keep me busy and my mind off girls. I called up my friend Joe to see if he had anything at Ultimate Athlete. It was all the way back home, a long drive from campus. But if this could make me happy, put me in a world where I was comfortable and getting me closer to a career, and keep me busy, then I had to at least check it out.

So, I went to visit Joe. He did not have anything at the moment for jobs, but he could create an internship for me. Over lunch we talked about all the possibilities we could do together. We discussed combining *Ultimate Athlete* with my nick name *Miracle Kid* to help sell the name. He put me in charge of marketing, getting our name out to the public, and editing the articles he wanted to post on his website. I could now get credit towards graduation by interning with Joe over winter break. During the fall semester Joe would send me articles and tell me they needed "more mustard," so I would review them when I returned home for the weekend. I liked to help Joe, because I felt like I was accomplishing something. The great thing about this was that I felt like it helped my journalism skills, while helping my knowledge of personal training.

We also worked on a new nutrition plan I felt worked really well. It's essentially called The Caveman Diet. The goal is to eat like a caveman. If it was here 10,000 years ago you can eat it. The diet contained meat, nuts, fruits, vegetables, and very little starch. You could not have any refined sugar, no bread, and no dairy products. This was the best diet I have come across yet.

For Columbus day break a group of friends invited me to a party in Fitchburg, MA, There was a pretty girl surrounded by all these guys who were talking to her. After the guys started to move elsewhere, I waited, played it cool and walked up to her and offered her one of Derek's beers. We hit it off instantly; her name was Julie. For three hours we talked about the joke I have with Derek and Jon that I'm 1% Puerto Rican and 1% black. We talked about my love for reggaeton. She thought it was the coolest thing. Then she said the famous words I get so often from everyone. "I know you from somewhere." Yup, I would say, I was the Miracle Kid. I could not escape it when I was in or around Leominster.

I wasn't going to hold anything back. I told her everything; the book I was writing, anything she wanted to know about my accident, and who I was as a person. Later when I asked her to the Olive Garden I said, "I'm not like most guys who want to have sex with you the first night I meet you. I'd like to get to know you. You seem like a really good person." Say what you want, but it worked and she said yes. The whole reason I decided to not hold anything back goes back to when Teddy Bruschi said be proud you are a survivor. I did just that.

We went to the Olive Garden and it just happened to be her favorite place to go. We had so much in common it was ridiculous; she was an athlete as was I, she was Latina . . . I pretended I was latino. We had many small ideals in common, and when I would say something she would respond, often, that she was thinking the same thing. After the date I asked if she wanted to go to my house and we could drive around listening to reggaeton. She was down for it. We had a blast singing along to the words of the songs, and admittedly she was a little better than I.

We hung out one last time before I went back to school. I drove to her house because she was not feeling well. We were on her computers and wrote things in Spanish to each other on our Facebook walls. I was excited that I was finally learning the Spanish language.

I drove back to school that night, excited the whole way because she was perfect in every aspect. She texted me before I got back to UMass to wish me luck while I was driving. She actually seemed like she really cared about me. She texted me all the time, sent me frequent messages on Facebook. I just prayed to God that this was real and that I had actually found a girl.

The day after my first date with Julie, Mom said that my dad had something to talk with me about. I had a feeling that both my parents liked Julie when they first met her. They didn't want me to mess up things. So my dad explained how to date after high school.

Dad   "what are your top priorities right now?"
Me   "the gym, and my internship"
Dad   "Don't change it, now that there was a girl in the picture."

Nobody had ever explained it to me like this before I needed it. But it didn't help.

Now I could date properly and not scare off any girls. This was all I needed to hear. As I had to learn everything over again, I needed to find those ways to mature.

As I was beginning to see Julie, I had just started going to church again. Not like most though. I went to meditate and clear my mind, be one with God. Often I would be the only one in the church. I would thank God for everything he has done for me, for saving my life, for everything he had done for my family. Of course, I would pray for Julie because she became sick with mono, and I prayed it would work out for us. I told him I just couldn't deal with another disappointment. There, in the church, I would sit in a pew and shut my eyes; with my hands together on my lap. I would in vision sitting with God, Jesus, and my grandfather. It was almost like we would sit there and I knew we were having a conversation but wouldn't hear any words. Just because I was with God, Jesus, and my diseased grandfather I found peace, that's all I needed/wanted.

At the same time I met Julie, my friends from back home who all went to college for a couple years started to come back to Leominster. So whenever I would go home they would always ask me to hangout. I didn't mind hanging out with them once in awhile, but they had a knack for finding trouble. I was starting to get my life together, and my friends tried to drag me into a life I left behind. I am different now. I wanted a job, to find a girl, start making some money. I had my priorities, but my friends did not. They wanted to have fun while they still could then settle down. I differed. I wanted to straighten out my life and take the occasional vacation.

Skyping with Julie was always an adventure. We spend hours talking at our computers. We would Skype until she was falling asleep. Many nights she would be dozing off as we talked. "I don't want to go to sleep, I want to talk to you." She would say. I would reply with a chuckle, "You need to go to sleep, you're too tired to talk."

There was one minor problem with Julie. Of course there was, you say. She was semi-involved with another guy. I had to stay positive because though I was beginning to like her a lot, and she was giving me signs that she liked me, I could set myself up to get hurt because I could not figure out how to deal with emotions. My brain could easy think I was in love when in reality I just had a friendship with Julie. This is why I developed such an obsession with Dianne. When I saw a girl who had all the qualities I desired in a girl, I would instantly fall in love.

Julie told me that all her friends hated her ex and she seemed to really like me. My brain really was warning me to take it easy, couldn't take more disappointment or confusion. Everything was in place. I just had to be patient and wait . . . again.

I got a job on the dining common washing dishes. It kept me busy, paid me, and I got to work on my hand-eye coordination with my left hand. I would often be in charge of grabbing the cups off the trays as they went by on the motorized rack. I would practice grabbing the cups with my left hand.

At the same time, this Pilipino girl IM'ed via Facebook. She said Happy Halloween and I asked her where I knew her from. She replied the Philippines and I told her that I had never been. We chatted for an hour straight. She started to ask me questions like if I had a fiancé and things like that. "She just wants citizenship to America," I joked to myself. But at the same time I thought this was great. Now, I don't have worry about Julie. I can just chat with Michelly and see what happens. If things didn't work out between me and Julie, I'll see what's up with this girl. I thought it was pretty good having a friend from a different country who would message you all the time.

Then her gay (literally) cousin wanted to be my friend on Facebook. He grew defensive any time he thought I was getting suspicious of his sexual orientation. I didn't care but I would just laugh and think how my life would make a comedy and a tragedy of a movie someday because of everything that had happened to me. In a matter of days I had two Internet pen pals on the opposite side of the world.

I had already experienced the absolute worse that life had offer, it could only get better from here. I had to be patient and let things happened. Whether it was getting my story out there and talking to people about the powers of God, or being able to play baseball again, I just knew there was a reason me being here. I had finally gotten to the point where I was content with my life and happy all the time. I went to a party at UMass and my friend Yogel said, "When I grow up I want to be you." I couldn't believe I was having this kind of effect on people. I was always happy, always laughing. I loved life and was so happy God had given me another chance at it.

My mother would text me at times and would say that she and my dad were proud of me. I would respond, "What for? I haven't done anything yet."

She would respond, "You are working plus going to school and going to the gym. Many people wouldn't do that."

To me, if you wanted something you had to work for it. I wanted money, I had to get a job. To make sure I had a job out of college I had to do an internship. I wanted a degree, I had to go to school. I wanted a nice body, I had to go to the gym. This was all part of something bigger. I knew if I put in the work now it would all pay off. I knew if I worked hard when I couldn't walk, it would pay off. I was close to a normal kid now.

I obtained this job and was passing school. Things were great, with this job came a sense of urgency I did not possess before. Because I had to work certain nights I had to do my homework whenever I could. I could no longer complete the homework whenever I felt like it. Of course, a couple weeks after my job began my professors decided to assign a ton of work due before Thanksgiving break. I found myself staying in on Friday nights to catch up, which I didn't mind. I was getting bored of the same old college routine and it gave me a chance to do my laundry. I was swamped with school work, but I had to keep working because I had things that needed to be paid off. Like a concert with Julie. I decided to extend an invitation to Julie via Skype; to see Aventura, a latino Bachata band in late November.

At this point in my recovery, after I do something that consists of a lot of mental work, I need to take a nap right after. I grow completely exhausted I start not being able to focus and the words on the paper becomes blurry. When I started getting swamped with school and would have several papers due, I would write one or two paragraphs and then take a nap. I would also avoid Skyping with Julie or Michelly before I wrote my papers as the conversation made me tired.

Eventually I finally passed in all my work, maintained my job, and now it was time for vacation. I had a hell of a vacation planned because it was Thanksgiving, my birthday, and I was taking Julie to a concert. I could relax as I didn't have to worry about school work.

Thanksgiving was just another Thanksgiving, but the day was my twenty-first birthday. All my close friends, people I practically consider family, came out to celebrate with me. We had Jon and Derek, obviously. My really good friend Travis Marcoux who was a close friend since we were in grade school. We also had Adam Sanchez and Jon Rodriguez. These were the friends who would be friends for as long as I was alive. The best part was when the night started off, my parents came out with us and bought everyone the first two rounds. Derek's Mom, Tonja, joined us. She said she couldn't miss one of her baby's birthdays.

I thought now, I could drink but while in rehab, the doctors and nurses would tell me if I drank alcohol that I would forget how to walk. This is good enough reason alone not to drink. By now I realized that this just wasn't the case, I could test the waters when it came to alcohol and be okay.

After our first two drinks, and after I made a fool out of myself on the dance floor, it was time to go out with just the guys. I didn't want Julie to come because I just wanted to be with the guys. We went to this Chinese restaurant called Singapore. It was awesome. I knew a ton of people there so everyone bought me drinks. I was having a great time being drunk, finally. I wasn't too paranoid to get drunk, and I wasn't scared like I used to be when I started drinking after my accident. I had worked hard enough in the gym that I gained back most of my coordination and balance back. My doctor does not encourage me to drink. She says this because it is toxic to the brain.

My friends and I walked to the back of the bar. I started saying hello to everyone, then I saw Natasha. She was a bitch to me last year when we broke up. The only words I said to her were "What's up?" I gave her a half ass hug and as I walked away I asked how she was without really waiting for an answer. Later that night my friend Annie asked, "Why didn't you get back to my happy birthday text?"

"I didn't get back to anyone."

"I know you didn't get back to Natasha's, we thought you would have."

"Why?"

And the conversation ended. When I woke up the next morning, and shook the hangover off, I felt a great deal of satisfaction. I was standing up for myself and with confidence. I didn't have to be nice to Natasha because she acted nice to me I knew she didn't care about me deep inside. She was only putting on a show. No more having girls step all over me.

The whole month of November I didn't see Julie. We texted everyday with the occasional Skype session. I had asked her in the end of October to come with me to an Aventura concert. She had said yes, but I still wasn't sure if she would be able to because her parents were very strict. The week before the concert her dad who was very old needed to have surgery. His neck swelled up to dangerous levels, and I thought Julie wasn't going.

Julie ended up being able to go. I was the only white person in line, but it was something I was used to. I was always the minority surrounded by minorities. My obsession with Latinas was in full blast at the concert. Everywhere I looked there was a beautiful Latina woman. I had so much fun at the concert, but I forgot that when the band talked they would talk in Spanish. And all of their jokes were in Spanish. When everyone laughed I would laugh too although I had no idea what they were saying. I tried to use the little Spanish that I could to translate, but that didn't work. For all I knew every joke was about the white boy in the audience who laughed at every joke.

When we pulled up to my house I used that I took her to the concert as an excuse to get a kiss. "Dame un beso", means give me a kiss in Spanish. As I said this I pointed to my cheek. She jumped at the opportunity to give me that kiss. Then she kissed me again on the cheek as we hugged and said our goodbyes.

Now that I was 21, I had to worry about my drinking problem, and drinking and driving again. The temptation was so great to do so. When I went to a bar I would often be the DD and many people would offer a drink. They would encourage me to have just one or two, but I wouldn't allow myself. I did not want to drink a little bit and drive because it would only lead to drinking a lot and trying to drive. Plus, I didn't mind not spending my money on alcohol.

Probably the biggest reason why I didn't drink was because I did not think that my brain could handle it. I believed it better to get drunk every once in awhile then to have a couple of drinks every night or every weekend. It scared me too much to take my life for granted again like I had when I was younger. I was older, knew what I wanted, and was wiser than when I was 17 and decided to get in the car and drive that night.

I had too much to live for now to make the same mistake twice.

Julie and I didn't last too long after that. I felt like she was playing games with me a lot. Like playing hard to get and it seemed like she was caught up in the whole college experience thing. But honestly I think I was just being paranoid because girls in the past always played some sort of game with me and lead me on. I didn't like how was always hoping that she'd text me back and stuff like that. So immediately after the concert I stopped having all contact with her. With this being said I continued to meet girls.

Then I met this short African American girl named Cynthia at a party at UMass right before winter break. She was a softball player at UMass and seemed like a safe bet. You know, good personality, cute, athletic, a lot of fun.

When winter break rolled around, I planned to go to Miami with my boy Ced to visit Cozzo. During my there I rediscovered the one gift that I possessed that was not taken away in the accident. My personality, or my frontal lobe, was not affected by the accident. I made everyone laugh and helped them enjoy life while we visited FSU. Everyone said that I was the funniest kid they had ever met and I should try a career in comedy. I now thought about the option of being a comedian. Life wouldn't be easy, but it was something I would enjoy doing. I had plenty of time to make a decision.

One thing was obvious. I had to move out of the cold and get into warmer weather. I could not take the extreme seasons of the New England climate any more. It was "cold" in Miami when I went down, and it was only 50 degrees. If I moved down here I wouldn't have to worry about blankets of ice and losing my balance and falling, which happened oh so much my freshman year of college.

CHAPTER 12

CONFUSION

After I returned from break, I was really getting into the stand-up comic idea. I did a lot of research on it. Not only did I research how to become a stand-up comic, but I wrote down anything that happened to me that I thought was funny, or maybe a joke or two that I would think of. For example, my teacher's zipper was open and I looked up in the middle of class and sure enough his penis was hanging out. I thought I should be a comedian because the things in my life that happened to me were funny and strange, and see them in this quirky way I can relate to others. This stand-up thing gave me something to strive for. This was a hobby, maybe a career, I could do my own thing and have fun doing it.

Although I had this new found interest in comedy, I often wished I could hit a restart button and just start my life all over again. Even though my life kept getting better and I thanked God I was alive, I wished that I could live my life over again knowing what I know now. I didn't have that many close friends like I thought I had before, and it seemed like my life had no order. Like it was upside down. My life was so good and had order in high school. Now, I just wanted some type of order and to stop having things change all the time.

I was eating in one of the dinning commons at UMass one afternoon when I looked up and saw a flier for a "Last Comic Standing" event. I thought, "Wow, this is perfect timing." I was beginning to get into comedy, see myself as a stand-up comedian, and then I see this flier. But I needed to get more information before registering. I wasn't sure if I could win, but this would definitely be a great experience.

I thought of different types of material to put into my act. I had some funny non-accident related stuff, but I could think of so many accident related things that were funny. I didn't think now would be the best time to talk about my accident, it being my very first appearance, but maybe down the road I could incorporate my accident into comedy and educate people about my story. I was pretty excited to do this show. The only thing I was nervous about was if I had good material or not. Presenting it, that was the easy part. I had to ensure I had something funny to say.

Cynthia turned out to be a lesbian. She told me she was bisexual, but in fact she was more attracted to women than men. She said I was the only man she was attracted too. We still remained good friends, but I was sick of this. I just wanted ONE good girl that I could chill with. None of this dating lesbians stuff or girls just using me for a hook-up. I wanted a girl friend! The problem was that every girl didn't want anything serious with anyone. They were interested only in themselves and just wanted to hook-up with guys or just wanted to be "friends." Any girl that told me that we were "best friends" I ignored. I am a relationship kind of guy, I have always been in a relationship, and I felt most comfortable in one.

One issue still harassing me was when it was cold people would approach and ask if I was OK or what happened to my leg. It seemed I would never escape the questions. I know it was just people who cared making sure I was OK, but it sucked. In my mind I was pretty much normal again. But when it was cold something happened to my muscles and I couldn't use them properly. This motivated me greatly to get out of the cold weather; my body just didn't work properly in the cold. My doctor believes that my limp develops when it's cold because of an injury I may have sustained in my accident. She says I may have hurt my hip or back this maybe true but I believe otherwise.

Even though I knew better, and fought against it, I began to visualize myself playing baseball next year because of how healthy I was getting. I told myself to ignore the feeling because I was setting myself up for another failed attempt. Even with my new found infactuation with comedy, I still wanted to play baseball.

Right around this time, I received a text from my mom that Mike, my lil bro, had made the baseball team at WPI (Worcestor Polytechnic Institute). I had nothing but feelings of joy for him. I was so happy because he worked hard the winter break leading into tryouts. I was also happy with myself because I had no feelings of jealousy. I did not say even to myself, "That should be me out there not him." As soon as I received the text from my mother, I quickly sent my bro a text saying, "congrats bro."

Derek was moving to Dallas. I was happy for him no doubt, but it was bittersweet. We had been through so much together, and now my one of my brothers was moving away. I then considered joining him. I thought maybe I could graduate from UMass, get my PT certification then move down to Texas and Derek could hold me down until I found a job personal training. I wanted to get away from Leominster so this would be the perfect way to do so. This was a backup plan of course, everything is subject to change if you meet a girl or get a job; you can't plan out exactly how life is going to go.

My parents took me out to eat that same night. They talked about how proud of my brother they were that he made the team. My mom said she was hesitant to tell me because playing in college was something I always wanted to do. My brother was never really sure if he wanted to play or not. I simply responded, "Shit happens," shrugged my shoulders and continued eating my steak tips. At this moment I started seeing the accident as a blessing in disguise. I would have never given up on playing baseball. I believe I would have never learned how to give up on playing baseball if I wasn't forced to like this accident made me do. If I was not forced to give up baseball, I would have never gave it up. I would of stopped at nothing to play in the majors.

Of course, I met this girl who worked in the dining common with me. She had developed a rather cute crush on me. I talked to her whenever I worked and she was a really cool and fun person to be with. I thought this girl was so cute she was absolutely adorable, you know? She struck me as the wife type. Oh, I forgot the most important details; I had a thing for short girls She was 5' 0" and the most important detail, she was Vietnamese. She moved to the states when she was twelve. I was over Latinas. Though beautiful, I just couldn't deal with the head games, I thought Asian women were the way to go.

Her name was Van, pronounced Von. When we hung out for the first time I took her to a party. She was only a senior in high school, 18, but she only hung out with family members who were older and in college. All the football guys on the UMass team thought she looked good. I got plenty of comments about her. She followed me around the whole night; she liked me so much it was so cute. I felt I had found something really good with Van.

When I started to date Van, I was so confused how to go about it. I wasn't sure if things acceptable in my culture would be acceptable in her Vietnamese culture I enjoyed learning about our differences, although it confused me those first couple of weeks. For example, she never looked for a kiss. When we hugged she would hug with all her might, yet she never wanted to cuddle. I began to see that for her to want to do those things, she would have to be my "girl." We'd have to have more of a commitment, not just the girl who I am dating to 'see how it goes.'

Shortly after I started things with Van, I took another road trip with Travis to Washington D.C., to visit my friend Thomas. I had a better experience there than I had the last time falling down the concrete stairs. I was now able to drink whenever I wanted without abusing it like I had in the past. I was better behaved than when I was younger. Sometimes I would start drinking only to realize how much I actually hated it and put it down.

I started to drink more often just to relax. It was nice to forget about how hard life was and everything I had been through. I just had to make sure I didn't over do it, and that the old Zach didn't come back.

In the gym I noticed that I didn't have to kill myself to get the same results. I felt that I was over-tired from working so hard immediately after the accident. I had to though in order to fully recover. When I was working out now, I stopped killing myself and concentrated on lifting. I did a lot less cardio than I was doing and just focused on getting stronger.

A lot of my not doing cardio was due to the fact that I didn't feel like it. I blamed the weather for my lack of cardio. When I got to the gym I was always freezing. It was always beyond windy in the Pioneer Valley in which UMass was located. Not to mention the genius who drew the layout of my school got the plans from a school designed for Arizona and essentially created one giant wind tunnel. Everywhere you walked, didn't matter what way, the wind always blew directly in your face. Not a gentle breeze either. A large gust of wind every single day. It was hard to begin my treadmill workout because I felt like my muscles were frozen. It almost felt like my brain could not send the signals to my body because the nerves were frozen. I always had mucus leaking out of my nose while I was on the treadmill forcing me to get off and wipe it off.

Right before spring break of my junior year in college I started realizing that my needing/ wanting an exotic girl was just a phase. It was just something I had to experience. I know this sounds funny, but I started to find white girls attractive again. And I found myself wanting a white girl. I think after I had some bad experiences with exotic girls it may have helped me get over all the bad experiences I had with white girls. But now I wasn't ruling out anything. Now, unlike before, I was left my mind open to everything and everyone. I still wanted a Latina because I loved the Spanish culture, and I wanted to be able to speak Spanish a little better than I could. Everyone who worked with me in the dinning common was Latino. I would often talk Spanish with them, but I had a mean case of Spanglish.

Its weird, I think this little phase I went through happened because of my accident. I was trying to find out who I really was. I felt like I didn't fit into the college life and I did everything in my power to try different cultural lifestyles. Then it hit me, I was trying to be someone else. I had to be Zachary Daniel Gauvin. I didn't need to identify with any culture or race, I could just be me. I didn't fit in with any one because no one is like me. I finally understood that I had to just 'do me' and I would find true happiness. When I finally started to do this and not care about what anyone thought of me because of the way I talked or the way I dressed, I was so comfortable, content, and happy.

Yet, at the same time, I couldn't have been more confused on where life was taking me. I still thought I was going to do something great with my life but I had no idea what. Between girls, baseball, school, work, the gym, and trying to figure out my career path, I was absolutely perplexed. I told Jhern how confused I was. He reminded me that I was not the only one. We were in college and this was the most confusing time in our lives. I was excited for Jon because he was doing great in football. At the offseason pro-day he ran a 4.4 forty. He was destined for greatness. I knew he would go far in football and always had his back when people would say things like "he's too small" or stuff like that. I knew he would be great.

I wanted to move to warmer weather and I loved the Latino culture. So Miami seemed the place to go. Personal training not only interested me, but I could get a job anywhere. I still wanted to try standup comedy, but I figured if I was meant to be a standup comic, it'll find me. Same with baseball. If I was meant to play I would know it. I wanted to be able to focus on one thing.

I was online one afternoon and those annoying pop-ups filled my screen. One of them was AmoLatina.com. Well, I love Latinas, so I clicked on it. It was a site dedicated to finding wives from Latin America for men in the U.S.. I thought it would be pretty cool to have a Latino wife who only spoke Spanish. This way I would be forced to learn Spanish to communicate with her. So I made a profile, updated a picture, and added girls to my favorites list. Now, I was all set. Whenever I was ready to get a wife I could just go on this site, start up some convos and be on my way. But this was just a backup plan. At this time I was buried in work, school work that is. I would get these headaches that would be like nothing I had ever felt before. All the concentration I was doing, even if I was just sitting in class, took a huge toll on my energy. My Web writing journalism class took the most out of me. I couldn't stare at a computer screen for an extended amount of time. It was a two hour class. Every day in this class I would get a headache and be useless the rest of the day. The thing that sucked the most was that I had a WWII class a couple hours after. I loved that class, but I couldn't concentrate in it. I would be so tired that I often had to leave to go to bed or go to church to meditate. Often, I couldn't even make it to church.

My web writing teacher often grew mad at me. He wanted me to set up interviews and it would seem like I was being lazy, but in reality I couldn't focus or concentrate. My brain demanded I get some rest for it.

I didn't do as well as I should have in my WWII class because I couldn't retain the information given in lecture. I had to leave early almost every class for a nap. I hated this because I loved everything about WWII. My father was teaching me about it since I was very young. He collected German SS helmets, and anything from the WWII era for that matter.

If I wanted to graduate on time I had to take 5 classes and right now I was only taking four and I was mentally drained.

One day I was checking emails and I had one that informed me my school mailbox was over-flowing. I quickly shuffled through all the mail and I came across not one but three letters that read OFFICIAL GOVERNMENT BUSINESS. At first I laughed and I said to myself, "This is a joke." Then I opened them.

I had missed my jury duty.

"Shit! Can't you go to jail for that?" I asked my friend Samone who helped me open all my letters. She chuckled and said, "Ya, but I would rather just pay a fine. Then you have that you went to prison on your record and you don't want that, even if it is two thousand dollars."

"What!? Two thousand dollars? I don't have two thousand dollars. I'll just go to prison . . . it can't be that long of a sentence."

I called my mom and told her everything that had happened. She told me to find a number to the Common Wealth of Massachusetts, Office of Jury Commissioner. I called Jon and had him shuffle through all the notices I had received in the mail to look for the number. After fifteen minutes of searching for the number, he told me to Google it. Just like that it popped up. I called it and the lady on the phone was real calm and asked me when I could make it. I set up a new court date a day after my finals.

I impressed myself. I wasn't even mad about the situation. Before, I would be pissed off and throw things or punch walls or dressers. I was beginning to be able to keep my temper under control. I remained calm throughout the whole situation.

As school grew closer to the end, my work grew increasingly difficult. I had all these things due at the same time and I felt overwhelmed. I knew the only way to get all this work done and done well was to pace myself and do it a little at a time. It seemed like I always had a headache. Jon would always ask if I was OK, telling me I looked miserable. I was miserable. I had a constant headache that would only get worse trying to do work and turn in work that was good enough to get a C.

My doctor tells me that the headaches I get are from my injury. It is my brains way to tell me that it needs to stop. People without brain injuries develop fatigue and grow tired. I grow tired as well but I develop a headache once my brain has had enough.

No one understood that I just wanted to be left alone when I had a headache. People would come up and talk and I would try to laugh with them or whatever, but in reality I just wanted to sleep. My brain felt like it was over-heated; it always felt this way after class. After class I would still have to go to work and do even more homework. The gym was the worst. I didn't want to be there. For the first time in my life I didn't want to go to the gym. I was burnt out.

As much as I hated school I made the best of it. I think I started to become more and more like my old self again. I stopped caring about every little thing and stop letting small things stress me out. It also helped that whenever I felt like drinking I could. I no longer had to worry about the after affect.

Being able to drink again helped because instead of being the sober one at the party I was able to relax and forget about the stresses of life. It was also easier to make friends. I always thought I was the friendliest kid ever, and I didn't need alcohol to make friends. But it is so much easier being on the same level as the other kids to make friends than when completely sober trying to communicate with drunken people.

I was sick of working out as hard as I did and not getting results. I saw an ad late one night for P90X after returning from a party.

I waited a couple of weeks to order it just to make sure that I still wanted it. Truth is, I was so excited to do it. I was bored with my current workout and this was a great way to change it up. This was the summer I could concentrate on doing whatever I wanted. I got a job working at a desk at a gym, had P90X to do, had classes to take so I could graduate on time, and near the end of school I found a tech school in Miami, Florida.

The school was called ATI and was a school that offered NASM personal training certification, which was the most sought after certification from employers. ATI help you get employed after you get your certification and they would help you a attain a job while you obtained your certification. This was the perfect way to get myself started in Miami. This also was the best way for me to get my certification. This was the best way for me to achieve my certification.

CHAPTER 13
MATURING/ GROWING UP

When I finished jury duty after it was postponed and then canceled on me several times, I came home to find that all my close friends were gone. They were spending their summer at school. Matt was in Rhode Island, Timmy was moving to Boston, Thomas was in Washington D.C., Travis was in Maine, Derek was in Dallas, and Jon was staying at UMass for the beginning part of the summer. I was in Leominster all by myself.

Everyone was really going their separate ways now. Everyone had their own life in different places. I thought my solution was that I needed to move as well. I too needed to move and get a new life of my own. I started to find ways to get out of this life I had here in Mass. I contemplated moving to Dallas with Derek and going to school. There was an ATI in Dallas. My parents sat me down and told me that most places require that you have at least one year job experience in the field for which you apply. My parents convinced me to stay. I could live at home for free, save up some money, and study for the exam and then move to wherever I wanted. I think the biggest reason I didn't want to move to Dallas that wasn't where I wanted to live. I wanted to live in Florida. I wanted live in South Florida. They convinced me this would be the quickest way to get me on my own in Florida.

I matured a lot during this part of my life. I had no one to influence my decisions. My friends were all off doing their own thing. So, that meant I was free to do mine. People in life come and go and you need to find your niche in society to be truly happy. I found it at the gym. I looked at other trainers, training their clients and said to myself this is what I want to do. I could do the thing I was best at all day, which was to interact with people. I could make them laugh and relax while putting them through a good, quality workout. This is what I wanted to do with my life. Be the highlight of someone else's day. I wanted to make other people's day better because they got a workout with me, and they enjoyed it.

When I saw that Ken Griffey JR retired, I was heartbroken. I grew up with him as my favorite player. I loved him and loved the way he played the game. He played the game as though he was still a kid. I live my life like I'm still a kid. Just because we grow up doesn't mean we can't have fun and laugh every second of every day of our lives. But when I saw that he had called it a career, that spoke to me. It is just a game and in the bigger scheme of things it really doesn't matter. So if Griffey could call it quits so could I. I was done pursuing my dream of playing baseball I was recruited by division one schools. That was good enough for me. Time to move on.

P90X was awesome. They were awesome workouts and I was learning a ton about fitness and personal training. The workouts were extremely intense. Another thing I liked was that they were so intense they only lasted an hour. I liked the mentality of get in, do what ya need to do, and get out. Yet, I was still stressing about my body. I was not getting fast enough results. Tony's saying, "Do your best and forget the rest" stuck with me and helped. I was skeptical if I was doing the moves wrong or right because my coordination wasn't perfect from my accident. I don't know if my coordination improved, but balance definitely did.

I started working at the health club way too much. In two weeks I worked 83 hours and tried to follow the P90X nutrition guide but I just couldn't. I would have been able to do it, but I didn't have a set schedule. I worked so many hours by covering people's shifts. I worked at all times at all different hours. I couldn't figure out a set schedule to work-out and I definitely couldn't eat right. If I couldn't do it right I'm wasn't going to get the results that I wanted. So there was no point in doing it. But I had learned a great deal and I brought that with me to the gym whenever I was able to get there.

Once I started working so many hours, I got addicted to money. I couldn't get enough of it. I watched the movie Empire and it's all about getting money and how in life the only thing that matters is getting money. This is true in a sense. Baseball doesn't matter, money matters. If I make a good living, my family would be able to live a good life and I would be able to enjoy it. I started looking into buying real estate in Miami and renting out homes. This income plus what I would make as a personal trainer would be plenty. And I could always buy more homes and rent them out, but I didn't think that I wanted to deal with tenants not paying rent.

I met Brittany through a mutual friend. She was cute and she was half Pilipino and half white. I was very attracted to her. I knew she liked me because every time she saw me she would stop whatever she was doing to give me a hug. I had my friend ask her what was up. She told him that she liked me but she didn't like the age difference. I just laughed and said to myself, "God really doesn't want me to have a girlfriend, does he?"

I needed to stop trying to be someone that everyone else wanted me to be. It was my life. I needed to just be happy. You start a relationship with someone because of the kind of person they are, not because of what they look like. Trying to find a girl with dark hair and nice tan skin was completely irrelevant to finding happiness. The same applied to where I wanted to move. I needed to find what worked for me. Due to my car accident, my nerves were all messed up and I reacted poorly to intense winters and intense summers. With the summer heat I would get dizzy and fatigued easily; with winter I could not move properly. My joints and muscles would freeze up.

I needed to move to a place with the best of both worlds. I didn't need to move to L.A., with Cozzo so that I could become famous. I needed to walk my own path. God saved me for a reason, and I believe it was to educate everyone on the dangers of drinking and driving and about TBI's. I also wanted to write as a way of telling my story, and I could write from anywhere. I also wanted to be a personal trainer and at this point in my life I already had close to ten grand saved up to buy a condo or townhome down south. I If I went to L.A. I would waste all that money.

I began to look at Virginia and the Carolinas. These areas are a great place to get all four seasons without the extremities of New England or Miami. I had a really good thing going with my job at the health club. I could train for a couple years, save up money and build up my resume until I was ready to move.

I started working summer camp at my health club. In the summer camp, I was a counselor who helped teach swim lessons and I would play football with kids. I would work a double shift on Wednesdays and Fridays. I had to take naps between my two shifts on Fridays and took naps whenever I could the rest of the days. One day I would work 6 a.m.

to 4 p.m., and I would be exhausted. I would come home and crash or I would still have to get to the gym so I would force myself.

My mom would often tell me to go watch one of the legion baseball games. I told her I didn't want to. That I just needed a break from baseball. She did not understand I needed a mental break from baseball. She also didn't understand the emotional toll baseball had taken on me, but no one could understand. Hell, I couldn't understand. I was so happy and content with my life, I didn't want a stupid game to change that.

Often, when I worked the camp, the kids would ask why I had so many scars on my body. They would be like, "What is that?" pointing to my throat, at the scar where I had a trach. I would answer car accident then walk away because I did not want to have to explain the accident, nor all the injuries I had received because after every day of this it gets old. One kid, Ryan who was about 9 years old; was getting ready to go down the slide into the pool. He just straight up asked me, "Why do you have so many holes in your body?" I laughed at the bluntness of his comment.

During my days at the camp, I noticed a lifeguard/ camp counselor who always had her eye on me. One day I sat next to her and started a little chit chat. Later that day she was bringing the kids to Roll on America, a roller skating rink the camp used. She kept telling me how I should go with them. I could tell she wanted to get to know me and I her. We brought the kids to Roll on America and when the kids ran off to skate we hung out. She bought me food because I didn't have money. When we got back Orchard Hills we left, not thinking anything of it. I had given her my number and she hit me up later that day to tell me that she had gotten yelled at by our camp director Bucky for leaving early (it was my fault because I told her that we could leave, don't worry I got yelled at too).

She was 17 years old and I was 21, but it was completely innocent. I didn't want anything from her nor did she from me. We were just friends who were attracted to each other. She was a half Italian, half Irish. The Italian in her was very attractive. While that wasn't the most important thing to me anymore, all I wanted was a good girl, I still loved that dark skin.

Her name was Taylor. The age difference became evident when she began to play little games with me to make me jealous. She would flirt with the other male counselor at the camp and started to ignore me. After a couple of tries to hang with her, I gave up. I wasn't going to text someone who wasn't going to get back to me or someone who would purposely flirt right in front of me and check to see if I was looking.

I became extremely paranoid. Why does every girl do this? What is going on? These were just a sampling of the things that ran through my mind. I started to stress out. I wanted a girl so bad but every little thing they did I would let get to me.

A new personal trainer was hired at my gym and I began to talk to him about his certification. Derek told me that he went through ISSA. It was all online including the exam, which excited me. I did not test very well. I looked at the ISSA website and like what I saw. There were different certifications I looked into. The personal fitness trainer certification (obviously), and there was one for nutrition—a fitness nutrition certification. I thought this would make me a well-rounded personal trainer and it would be easier to obtain a job.

Yet even with paranoia setting in, I still felt that everything was coming together. The good news was that my paranoia was about a girl and that could easily be fixed. I heard this quote in a movie over the summer and it made me think, it went something like this; You will always lose money chasing women, but you will never lose women chasing money.

So I thought up of ways to make more money, but in a way that I would be happy. I started seeing the best way for me to make a future for myself. I thought maybe I wouldn't move away from Leominster right away, but maybe I would stay here and personal train clients while beginning to promote myself as one who could help others with a similar condition to mine.

While I was working camp one day Brittney jumped out of the pool to talk to me. After we talked for a while I started to think maybe I cut this off too soon. She had a great personality and she had the dark features that I loved plus an extremely nice body. So I started to text her again and we made plans to go hangout by the pool at the health club one afternoon.

I had a lot of fun with Brittney when we went to the pool. We tanned for a little, played in the pool, went down the slide, and even played volleyball.

I began drinking a lot that summer and wasn't working out the way I should have been. I drank often, not binge drinking, but it was more often than I had liked or anticipated.

And, I developed another addiction that would begin to show. Addicted to what you ask. Addicted to COOKIES. I loved cookies. I couldn't stop eating them. The worst part was my body looked absolutely fine. I would eat a whole carton of cookies, go out and have a couple

Mike's Hard Lemonade (I hated beer), and the next morning my body looked better than the day before. I thought maybe because I was stress free my body produced hardly any cortisol, which meant I didn't get fat because I wasn't stressing over what I was eating.

I started drinking Mike's Hard Lemonade because it tasted awesome. I didn't care what people thought. I would go to the bar and order a Mike's and people would stare at me and I would stare back. I hated the taste of beer. Mike's was delicious so I drank that. It did have more alcohol than beer, which scared me because I was starting to drink more often. I wasn't sure if my brain could handle all the alcohol. Yeah, I may have healed almost fully by now, but I still had to be cautious of what I put into my body. I was not like most people my age because of the injury I have sustained.

After I went to the pool with Brittney I went to the pool with my fiend JRod. Taylor was working again that day on life guard duty. The whole time I was there I caught her looking at me or she would try to talk to me. JRod went in to get changed and I sat out by the pool relaxing. I then heard a soft psssh. I opened my eyes to see who or what it was. Taylor was trying to get my attention from her lifeguard chair. She said something I couldn't hear so I walked to her. She wanted to do something that night. So we made plans but when I texted her later that day, I got no response. I couldn't see that she just wanted attention and was playing a game with me.

One of the hardest tasks to conquer when recovering from a brain injury is making sense of the motives of those around you. When you're with the opposite sex you may think that they like you or that there is a mutual attraction between you two, but that may not be the case. It's tough because you are learning everything all over again. When learning how to handle the opposite sex, you might as well be learning how to walk again.

I finally figured out how to handle girls. Back when I had no plan, no focus in my life, it was tough. I was looking to them as a replacement, something to give me purpose. But I had a job, a sure way into personal training, and I was finally able to get women out of my head as a main focus.

As summer was coming to a close I sent Coach Stone an email to update that I would not be able to tryout. It read:

Coach Stone;

I just wanted to let you know that I will not be in attendance
at this year's baseball tryouts. I have way to many things going
for me right now. I am working in a gym on Friday nights at
home, this is important to me because I want to be a personal
trainer. I also am writing a book about my accident and my
recovery which is taking up some time. I have 102 pages down
so you can see that I am taking it seriously. you are in it! I
want to thank you for being so supportive in helping meet my
desires although my dreams of never playing division 1 baseball
ever came true. I was to thank you for everything you have
done for me.

—Thank You Zach Gauvin

Even though I was never able to play Division 1 baseball for UMass,
I still felt I owed Coach Stone an email. I know he wasn't sitting on the
couch at home twiddling his thumbs asking himself where I was. But he
did a lot for me and he was a great guy.

Coach Stone replied:
Zach;

I'm glad that you are doing well and I appreciate your kind
words . . . . however, you have done everything to put yourself
in this great position. Keep going in the same direction that
you have been and you will be fine.

Good luck,
Coach

Mike Stone
Head Baseball Coach
UMass/Amherst

Just like that my dream of playing division 1 baseball had come to an
end.

CHAPTER 14

NEW ATTITUDE

I moved into UMASS early my senior year so I could set up my room properly. I had a single room again in John Quincy Adams (JQA), a dormitory in southwest. But one thing was different. Instead of living in the single room alone, I would have a roommate. That's right, two people living in a room meant for one. Jon was going to stay with me for the first semester so he could save some money.

We wanted to loft the bed over the futon to make more room. I gave Jon the desk and we had a nice little set up planned out. Lofting the bed, that was a process. Picture dumb and dumber trying to disarm a bomb. Jon had a learning disability and I had a brain injury. After gallons of sweat dripped off our faces, we finally set up the bed. Every night he would climb to the top bunk that had the mattress and sleep on the bed. I would sleep on the futon below; probably the most uncomfortable futon in the world. Metal bars ran through the mattress and I could feel their outline on my back and legs.

I didn't want to deal with climbing the ladder to get up on the bed every night because I had really sensitive feet. Not only were my feet super sensitive, but also my hands; I think that my nerves were heightened for some reason because of my injury. I couldn't stand on a hot surface for very long and I couldn't handle plates when they came out of the dishwasher because they were too hot.

My doctor tells me that my nerves may have been heightened but it is more likely that just the perception of stimulation had changed. Simply meaning I may think it is hotter than it actually is/ feels like. She said in time I may see improvement in this area.

I did all this for Jon because he was my friend and very much like family. Jon was going to need my help a lot this year so he could concentrate on football. I knew, especially at this school, no one was going to look out for him. People only seemed to care about themselves and their own immediate needs, at least in our circles. It's ridiculous, but that's not how I am or how I was raised. When you see someone in need and you can help them then why wouldn't you? It makes me mad to see the direction I sometimes think American society is going, but this is not me and I refuse to change. I'll help people out. I'll be the nice guy even if that means I get shit on by other people. That's all I know how to be.

The first game for Jon ended in victory for the Minutemen. Jon ran for 133 yards and had two catches for 60+ yards. He did it big and I was proud of him. It felt so weird, my pride was almost as if I was a father and he my son. but I would never show it. I couldn't let him get a big head. I believed if he knew he was that good his output on the field would decline. I would say to him, "Well you could do this better or I liked it when you did this." For example when I would see him after a game I would give him a hug and whisper in his ear "your slow ass should of had 3 touchdowns instead of 2." I would say this jokingly, knowing that this would make him work harder. I tried to help him out the best I could.

There were so many girls at UMass and every one of them beautiful. But I wasn't going to let them get to me. I would look at an attractive girl then turn away and remind myself, "There's no point. They are all only trouble and games." I once heard a quote that stuck with me, "Women cloud the mind." This couldn't be truer. I could be focusing on school, work, or sports and yet always subconsciously thinking of that girl I just saw or the women I pictured asking to be my girlfriend. One could have a clear mind and head on straight, then you meet someone and suddenly can't figure out how to put on your shirt.

My schedule was unbelievable busy. I was here, there, everywhere. I was going to school at UMass taking five courses. I had all my school work to do, I still had my job in the dinning common where I worked twice a week. Sunday night and Thursday night from 9 until 1 I would wash dishes for late night. I also kept my job working at Orchard Hills

Athletic Club on Friday nights in the fitness center. I would drive home to Leominster every Friday to work from 4-9 p.m. I would drive back on Saturday mornings in time for Jon's game. With all this going on I still was trying to help Jon as much as I could with rides, money, and whatever else he needed. This year was a crucial year for him to get seen by an NFL team. I wanted him to focus and not have to worry about money. On top of this, I still had to fit in getting to the gym three times a week so I could at least maintain what I had gained. I didn't want to get fat while concentrating on all this other stuff. Also, I was writing and revising my book. But all of these were passions of mine, things I wanted to do so it was much easier than if they were all things that I didn't care about. Except school, I could have done without school.

Roughly five years removed from my accident, I was still trying to walk with sandals correctly. After showers I would walk from the bathroom back to my dorm room. I still had to focus on landing my foot the proper way. I focused on the outside of my foot so I could keep my sandal from twisting sideways. It had to do with the way I walked or the way my foot landed. When I walked normal with sandals, the sandal would always end up crooked; instead of my foot landing directly on the shoe and staying straight.

I did well that early autumn not letting girls getting me off track from what I wanted to accomplish. It was time to focus on what I really wanted. I wanted to get bigger, just five or ten pounds on my frame. I thought that would be a sufficient look. My goals as you can tell are a little more realistic than before where I strived to get the perfect body all at once. I was able to lift a lot more than before and my left arm was stronger so I thought this was an accomplishable goal. Instead of getting my body even (my left side even with the right), I could focus on total strength. I would use both my right foot and left foot on an exercise machine at the same time. I immediately began to see results. I remember from my rehab that when I incorporated both hands in the exercise my weaker arm became stronger during the exercise. More strength = more size. I began to eat more just to take in more calories.

I began to see a difference at the gym immediately. I knew why too. Instead of caring what people thought and how much weight they could do in the gym compared to me, all I cared about was how I was doing in the gym. I focused my whole workout banging out rep after rep, set after set. I just thought to myself, "Yeah, I probably won't be able to bench more than my body weight on a standard bench, but that's not going to stop me." I had to find alternatives and incorporate them into my workout. Just using the machines were great. Now, that my left arm and leg were caught up (for the most part), I felt stronger than before my accident. Even my flexibility had improved. I'm not sure if that was from the yoga I had done in p90x this summer, but it was even better than when I was doing p90x.

The best part was I was getting compliments when I was with Jon. This was huge for my confidence. As you know, Jon had the perfect body because he had freak genetics and worked extremely hard. Now, instead of hearing "Wow, Jon you're getting pretty big." We heard, "You guys been hitting the gym? You both look really good."

See, my whole life I have been trying to get that perfect body. I care way to much about what people think about my appearance. I wanted to have something that no one else did, that way I could be proud of myself. But for some reason, may it be genetics or a poor diet, I could never achieve the body I wanted.

I figured out why I hated school so much. When I am in class or doing homework, I get bored and annoyed. I think to myself that I can find so many better things to do with my time. I didn't care about anything I was learning. I thought about how I could be getting my personal training certification or how I could be learning Spanish, but instead I was always in my dorm room a working with things I had no interest in.

Another reason I hated school so much was my brain was on constant overload. It always felt heavy, always hurt. I swear, I could feel my brain swell as I studied. By the time I was done studying/ doing my work, I couldn't think about anything. I honestly felt like I had no more room in my brain to think about any new things. It was like as I am studied someone opened my skull and jammed a bunch of stuff in it. I felt sluggish and could feel my mind work slower. It was a feeling I could easily do without. Imagine always feeling fatigued, having a constant headache, having a constant "full brain." I knew the best way to settle my brain was to nap, but I had no time. So, I did my best without naps but I would get these headaches almost every day. They were excruciating!

I would take Relpax and my headaches would fade gradually, until they disappeared. Relpax was a pill, prescribed by my doctor. Relpax would relieve me of my headache, but my head would still feel tired, fatigued.

My brain felt like it had just lost a war. Could it be that my brain was so badly damaged my head couldn't recover from a headache quickly or at all? I had no choice but to think this was possible. I couldn't think of any other reasonable explanation.

I used to ask a lot of questions in class. I knew people were annoyed by the amount of questions I asked, but I didn't care. During my first semester of my senior year I had these two professors who would just create random work for us to hand-in. It was nowhere to be found on the syllabus. I was so annoyed. Another reason for my head to hurt because I couldn't figure out what was due and when it was due. Most classes had a syllabus and everything was on there, but these two classes were ridiculous.

I would ask questions constantly to try and figure out what was going on. I didn't care if people found me annoying, I just didn't care what they thought at all. It was hard enough to try and keep up with what the professors were saying. One of my teachers talked so fast the students couldn't get a word in. But I kept asking questions. I had to take care of myself because no one was looking out for me. I was constantly asking myself when stuff was due and did I have enough time to do my work.

This stress led me to quit my job at the dinning common. I was only working two shifts, but one was on a Sunday when I did the majority of my homework for the week. With a brain injury you need to find a schedule that works for you and be able to plan out your day. I was still working my one shift a week at Orchard Hills. But for right now I was going to school to get my degree, not to work. These teachers were stressing me out, confusing me; I had to get a stress free schedule to pass my last hard semester of school.

I was in my dorm room with Jon one night. Jon was writing a paper and I was watching Saturday Night Live. The episode featured Shiloh Labeouf as the host. During one of his performances, he clapped extremely fast. I tried to repeat the action just as fast. I failed miserably. Instead of my clap being fluid and sounding like I was actually clapping, it was uneven and sounded like I couldn't connect my hands to make the clapping sound.

Jon turned around from typing his paper and asked what I was doing. I said "Nothing." But he just stared at me.

"Whenever I see people on T.V. doing something I have yet to master, I try to do it and see how much better I have gotten at it." Then he watched me attempt to do it again. He laughed hysterically at my attempt. I sat up and moved to the side of the bed. I kept trying to clap fast. My right hand would move as fast as I wanted, but my left hand would shake back and forth never hitting my right hand. I couldn't do it. It was something I had to practice to master, but just not important enough to actually practice. When would I actually need to clap at a high rate of speed?

My doctor said that I was not able to do this because the coordination of the brain had not yet fully healed.

All these little things that I still couldn't do that would make me a normal human being were just not important enough to stress over. I already had my rehab and that was hell for three or four years. I could get by without the things that I couldn't do perfectly so why would I bother myself with those tedious tasks? I don't need them to live a long, happy, successful life. That was how I coped with the small areas that reminded me of my brain injury. I didn't need those things.

I was taking a class called entrepreneur journalism that really taught me how to use the Web, especially Facebook and how to use social media to promote ideas. I made a Facebook group called Miracle Kid to let people know what I was doing, what I was thinking, and the projects I worked on. I then created a blog on Wordpress to see if somehow I could get the traffic from that site to my Facebook group. I thought back to my freshman year of high school where I sold condoms to anyone who wanted them. Kids were too shy to go in and buy condoms, so I would walk into CVS and buy the economy pack of condoms. It had like 30 something condoms in it and I would sell three for five dollars. I made LOOT!

As the final year of college went by, I started to going out more. On a Sunday night, Jon, my friend Rob and I went out. We were going up a couple floors in JQA to hang out with some girls. We needed to transport our alcohol some way. We needed a book bag and Rob wanted to take mine. I kept asking him if there was another way we could transport the alcohol. I was making a big deal out of it to the point that I was almost stressed because I knew I needed to have order and organization in my life and this would shake up things. Rob said that it wasn't a big deal and we used my book bag.

The next day, I was trying to get organized. Just because the book bag was on the floor instead of in my closet I couldn't figure out where anything went. I needed to be organized because if I wasn't I would forget where everything was. Just because that bag was out of place, I couldn't picture where anything else was! I was so confused; running my fingers through my hair, staring at nothing. It was so bad Jon asked if I was okay. But once I put that bag where it belonged, everything fell into place.

I loved my leg workouts! For leg press I had four forty fives on each side plus a twenty five on each side, plus whatever the machine weighed. It felt really good to blast my legs like this because in the past I had neglected my legs. I would run, but I would never lift heavy. I learned that you needed to lift heavy for your upper body to grow. This produced testosterone you wouldn't use otherwise.

There was one problem with me lifting legs so hard. My left leg would shake out of control and after a workout it was difficult to walk. I would lift so much weight on the leg press, I would end my workout and pretend I was in excruciating pain to explain why I was limping. I couldn't get away from the shaking. I thought by now that my shaking would cease, but that was not the case. I just had to stay with it and maybe one day it would go away.

Even with this problem, the best part of this stage of my recovery, compared to every other stage of my recovery, was the psychological aspect. I was beginning to believe in myself. I **BELIEVED** that I could do everything others could do. Unlike before where I would **THINK** that I could do something and I would fail at it. The mind is a very powerful thing and if you don't believe in what you are doing, then you won't succeed. It sounds harsh but it is true. If you don't believe in yourself, why should anyone else—or why should your body?

I started really trying in school, unlike before where I didn't try as hard as I could. I told myself I had a brain injury so there was no point in trying because I couldn't succeed. I wrote a paper for my political science class. I shut myself out to the world for about four hours. I turned my paper two weeks before the due date. When everyone was passing in their paper on the due date, the professor asked, "Is Zach Govaun here?" I raised my hand. The instructor said "Will you please come up and get your paper?" I walked up hoping I at least got a C. I snatched the paper from my professor's hand and took a quick glance.

A-

Wait . . . I couldn't believe my eyes. An A-? I walked back to my desk with a smirk on my face, as if getting an A- was my job, when in reality this was the first A- I received in college.

In October of my senior year, I still had a hard time watching the MLB postseason. I couldn't watch postseason baseball because I still got images of returning to the diamond. I'd want to watch, but I couldn't. I could only watch a couple innings before being forced to shut it off.

I was doing a good job not thinking about girls, but whenever I would think about girls I would tell myself I had to concentrate. Then, I would put on my headphones and play "Successful" by Drake. It would help me focus on what I wanted. I wanted money, cars and clothes. Then he would sing "the ho's, I suppose. I just want to be, I just want to be successful." I thought to myself, "This is all I want too." I would often see a girl and be like "Damn, I want that," but then I reminded myself, "Damn, I just want to be successful." Thoughts of being successful and doing great things ran through my head.

I have always had trouble drinking all types of liquids since my accident. To drink them without choking I developed a bad habit of blocking the hole of the beverage with my tongue to slow the liquid as it flowed into my mouth. If it flowed too fast I would always choke on the liquid because of the tracheotomy. My friends would make fun of me because they said it looked like I was French kissing the beverage.

I began to think about how to drink liquids. I could successfully drink beverage's out of a can, but bottles were a different story. The only time I would drink out of a bottle was at a party or when I went to a bar. I had to be careful drinking out of anything because if I tilted my head too far back as I drank, it would ensure that I would choke.

I kept getting headaches and migraines; vicious migraines. School was stressing me out, there was so much that I had to worry about plus going to class and listening to people talk about things I didn't care about for two and a half hours. Two and a half hours! There was one week where in five days I had four migraines. If I didn't take a pill in time, I couldn't do anything. The only thing I could do was keep my eyes closed and bury my head into the sleeve of my arm. Not to mention all the homework. That's why I tried to get my work done as soon as it was assigned because I didn't know when one of these terrible migraines would strike.

Even though I had finally rid myself of girls, there was always some girl who dangled like a tempting carrot. I met this girl Laura at the beginning of the school year. I took her out, we held hands and I even kissed her. We hung out once after that night and then I refocused on my book, school, work and everything else. So, I stopped talking to her. A month went by with no communication. Then I bumped into her at the dinning common. Her eyes lit up when she saw me and ran over to talk to me. After a month of not talking this girl still likes me.

We made plans to eat at the dinning common one night for dinner. We had dinner and it was obvious she was attracted to me, and I'll admit I was feeling her. We made plans to get dinner the next night too. I was on Facebook the next day and I had wondered why Laura hadn't friended me yet. I went to Laura's Facebook page and there it was, "In a relationship with . . . ." I couldn't believe it. She was in a relationship with someone else. So when she texted me and asked where I was so that we could meet and go to dinner, I didn't respond.

As long as I can remember I have wanted a tattoo that ran across my shoulder blades and was right below my neck. As I was reading a speech from JFK for one of political science classes in the summer I stumbled upon a quote that really grabbed my attention. The quote was a Bible passage from Isaiah 40:31. It read:

> but they that wait upon the LORD
> shall renew their strength.
> They will soar on wings like eagles;
> they will run and not grow weary,
> they will walk and not be faint.

I immediately wrote this on a piece of scrap paper at the health club where I was working. This quote is what I had done for so long. When times got hard I told myself, "It's okay, God's looking out for me. As long as I have God I'm good." Every time I wanted to quit, I would find God again and I renewed my strength. I would not give up.

Now that I had found what I wanted, I just wasn't in the mood to get a tattoo. I wasn't in the mood to sit for an hour with a needle being driven into my back. But, weirdly, I drove to the tattoo parlor anyway. It was like someone made up my mind for me and I had no choice. I got ISAIAH 40:31 across my back, in-between my shoulder blades in Old English font. I walked out of the shop as if nothing happened. I felt like it was something I had to do rather than something I wanted to do; a strange feeling.

I began to find numerous Facebook groups online; thousands of people dealing with the same thing I was. I began to friend these people and talk to them. They would ask me questions like "What do you think of this" or "What did you do think about that?" For example "What did you do when you had trouble sleeping." I would answer these questions as best as I could and as fast as I could. I even made a Facebook page called the Brain Injury Support Group and linked it to my blog. My blog was filled of tips that helped me recover or little tricks that helped me through my recovery.

My blog, Facebook page, and Facebook group were all doing very well in the first couple of weeks. I even had people all over the nation wanting me to post a link to their site or their blog to my site. I talked to this girl from England named Charlie every night about our injuries and the difficulties we faced.

I began to enjoy the process of writing. I started writing just to pass the time. One night in my dorm Jon was using the Internet (we had to share the outlet for the Internet—when he was plugged in I didn't have Internet and vise versa). I couldn't use the Internet and I didn't like anything one T.V. I thought about how I enjoyed writing. I started some short stories and books. Two of the stories were of my father, William, and the other was about my roommate Jon. They both had amazing lives so there was plenty of stuff to write about. I "based" it on their lives, so I could be as creative as I wished. The other two were stories based on characters I made up. These characters had a brain injury like me; the stories about events someone with a brain injury may encounter.

I was starting to make sense of everything. After all this time, four years, I was beginning to find my niche in society. I was beginning to feel comfortable.

I went to the gym one day and as I opened the door, I saw they had closed for good. I was extremely upset. Not because I didn't have any where to work out. I could always workout in my room or at the fitness center at UMass. I was upset because this was one place that I actually fit in. All the friendships I had made here were now gone. I would have to adjust all over again. I felt like the entire time I was at UMass I was stuck in recovery mode. It was terrible. It was almost like I didn't know how to make new friends when I was at school. All my friends were at the gym and my connection with them was terminated.

I also noticed over the years of my recovery I had developed trust issues. The only people I trusted were my parents. I felt like everyone else was out to get me, even Jon or my brother Mike. I would misplace something and instead of taking time to calm myself to find it, I would think, "I can't believe Mike would take that" or "I can't believe that Jon would take that." Many of my issues stemmed from trusting girls and believing what they said, leading me on only to find disappointment.

I was really beginning to help people with, and people dealing with, brain injuries. It made me so happy to help out. I was giving people with brain injuries a luxury I never had as I went through my recovery. My blog even attracted people studying brain injuries. A man who was conducting a study on speech and brain injuries came to me to help with his study. He was an electrical/computer engineering student focusing on a concentration in biomedical signal processing at Rowan University in New Jersey. With a few emails back and forth I gave him all the information I could. He wanted to know what kind of trouble I had with speech. I told them that when saying the letter s, instead of finishing with a strong sssss we would finish with a shhh, almost like were too lazy to finish the letter.

All the doctors think they can tell a patient with a TBI what to do to get better. Some of their tips work, but most of them just aren't what people are looking for. People need a first person account. I was giving out so much information that one person wrote this as a comment in these exact words. Remember, a lot of my readers have brain injuries:

"There are so many information online about brain supplements but for me this one is the most reliable. It gives specific information about the subject which is very important to us (readers). I really appreciate it and I hope you will post more. Thanks."

I also began to do research in publishing my book. I called a publishing consultant and asked for information from a self-publishing web site. The publishing consultant from that company called me a few days later. We talked about everything I wanted to do with my book, and then he said, "You keep 100% of your rights, so if you get a movie deal . . . ." He went on to say how it's a likely scenario. Of course, me being who I am, got way too excited and told everyone I came in contact with.

Finally the day had come for Jon and I to return the key to our college dorm. We were moving out for the semester. I exited JQA dormitory. I slammed the car door shut. Jon sat next to me in the passage seat of my Durango, munching on a sandwich. I fiddled with the radio until I found a song that brought joy to my ears. I stopped at a stop sign. Looked both ways then continued on my journey back home. I let out a loud yell of joy. "I'm finally leaving UMass, I'm done with this place!" Jon looks at me and just says, "Calm down dude." But I didn't care. I was moving on with my life.

When I returned to Leominster everything went my way. I didn't eat anything before I left UMass because I just wanted out of there. I began to get hungry on our way back. We stopped in my high school coach's insurance office to pick up the car my coach was going to let Jon use for the month he was home. We stayed and talked with Coach Decarolis, then he offered us Italian food. It was my lucky day! Waiting to eat was a terrific decision. Little things like that went my way all day. Everything would always go wrong at UMass. Nothing seemed to turn my way. But now, things were already going my way!

See the problem I had at UMass is I felt like was stuck recovering as I've mentioned. But another problem at UMass was that I was forced to grow up a lot faster than anyone my age. UMass was filled with kids trying to find out who they were, but I already knew who I was and what I had to do. I couldn't go out every night and get drunk. I had to take naps and go to sleep early, allowing my brain to heal. Leaving UMass, I would be able to make friends because I began a whole new chapter in my life. One more semester and I would rid myself of the "college experience" for good.

CHAPTER 15

RECOVERED

N ow, I may not be fully recovered or be "100%," and I may never fully recover. But I have recovered more than most people who attain this injury; lived when they said I wouldn't. I have hurdled the obstacles of both physical and mental torment and surpassed them to achieve greatness (graduating college, writing this book, helping people with brain injuries). I am able to live a normal, successful life now. I was forced to grow up much faster than any one my age. All those people who thought that I was a nobody, thought I was weird, or thought I was a creep because they judged me before they knew me, are going to be awestruck when they see I'm able to help thousands of people. What are they doing now?

I wrote a blog post about how I had trouble drinking liquids and swallowing. I wrote that you are supposed to angle your head down when swallowing as this helps direct food down the correct tube, it won't block your airways and you will avoid choking. One of the avid readers of my blog read this post. She was eating something juicy and started to choke. Remembering what I wrote, she tilted her head down and was able to swallow her food. She thanked me via Facebook over and over again. I was obviously happy that I indirectly saved her life, but it also felt good to help other brain injury vicitms with the struggles of everyday life.

The Saturday I returned home and went to the gym, I showed a personal trainer at the health club the blogs I created and managed. It immediately sparked her interest and she told me that she wanted one too. I offered her my services (for a price, of course), and told her I could create one for her. With my background in journalism I could manage it as well. Just like that, two days back from school, I already had a job offer in my field and I hadn't even graduated!

After I went to the gym and got the job offer, I wanted to look at cars. I went to the dealership to look at the sporty Honda CR-Z. I was disappointed as I looked in the window to see that it was just a two-seat vehicle. As I was leaving the dealership my friend Ray ran out of the Kia office and yelled my name. He came over and we started to talk. He told me that he had gotten a job with the Honda office. I asked why he had come out of the Kia office. It turned out the Boston Celtic's 2008 championship trophy was in there. Stunned, I began to walk toward the office. I ended up getting my picture taken with two of the girls on the Celtics dance team with the trophy in the foreground. "This is just my day," I said as I walked out of the office.

I started to get better at trusting people. I didn't feel like everyone was out to get me. I knew I had to trust people if I wanted to get anywhere in life. So I really put an emphasis on this. I reminded myself that not everyone is out to get me, there are good people out there.

December 28th our grades came in. I didn't know because I was done with school, I had left it behind, didn't want anything to do with it. I needed to pass all my classes in order to do my internship at Orchard Hills Athletic Club and graduate on time, but otherwise I didn't care. When I pulled up to my house after hours of shoveling at Orchard Hills, I walked into the front door. I saw my mother with tears in her eyes. She said, "Your grades came in." I immediately thought to myself, "Shit . . ." Then she exclaimed that I had gotten a 3.0 and passed all my classes. I was going to be able to do my internship and graduate on time. No extra years, no extra classes. My parents were thrilled. This was the best semester I ever had and I had received my first 4.0 in one class.

I stayed on top of all the classes I had to to pass. But if I didn't need to something in order to graduate, I didn't care. One thing that helped was taking classes I liked. For example, my magazine writing class and my entrepreneurial journalism class were both very interesting. I found them both helpful and useful. If I didn't care for a class, my law class for example, I did the bare minimum to pass. We wrote one paper that was worth 1/3rd our grade. I told myself that if I did well on it I'd be set. I got an A- and I was done in that class. From there all I had to do was get C's and D's on exams and I would pass. I hated school. I just wanted out. I refused to take pride in the work I handed in unless I liked the class. I don't know, call it ignorance, but nobody could understand what went on in my head. Not even me!

One night I was working the late shift at my gym until 10 or so. All the members of the administration went off to a meeting. They are usually gone by five at the latest. Every one of them seemed clearly sad about something, but they were not giving up any information. Paul (the employee working the front desk) and I could only speculate what had happened. We both were getting a vibe that someone had died. The vibe that was put out by everyone, it just felt like someone had died.

I had to work again at six in the morning the next day. When I got there all the members of the administration were there again. They usually don't come in until eight. Cindy, the general manager, gave me a "Hey, Zachy Zach!" I knew something was up and they just weren't telling me. It wasn't until later that I found out the owner of the club had died. He was in good health. I always saw him working out. He was seventy years old, however, but in great shape. This made me think that I had to be destined for something. The owner was in great shape and he randomly passed away one day. I screw up big time, go through hell, and I'm fine.

I go to the bar one night and see my friend Johnny P. He was excited because I do not see him very often. We sit and talk about life for a little bit. Johnny tells me, while sipping his beer, "My aunt believes in God because of you." Shocked by this statement, I leaned in closer to better my hearing in the loud bar. Johnny's mom worked in the I.C.U., the night of my accident and witnessed me at my worse. He said, "My aunt says there is no medical explanation why you're alive, no one has came in worse and no one is doing as well as you are." Jonny says he uses me as an example to all his friends when they complain about life. He says to them, "If you think your life sucks and you can't overcome it then look at my friend Zach."

I hated school so much I decided to intern at Orchard Hills in my finally semester. During my time there, I had many things to accomplish. I had to create and maintain a blog for Orchard Hills and be a one-on-one aid for a student enrolled in a life skills program at West Boylston High School. I had to maintain Judy's blog, maintain my own blog/ Facebook page, and finish my writing projects. I was also studying for my personal training certification during this time. All of this was new to me, I was finally doing my own thing. Things that I wanted to do. I must admit it was kind of weird not having Jon live with me or seeing him every day, but I enjoyed the break. I felt like I could finally grow as an individual. But even without Jon I was surrounded by good—no great—people.

Will worked the front desk at the gym where I interned. He treated everyone as if they were his favorite person in the world. So friendly and nice to everyone he came in contact with. This is exactly how I used to be, before my injury, before college. At UMASS everyone only cared about themselves. Because I was relearning how to treat people and interact with them, I learned to only care about myself. This backfired and I ended up alienating myself, confused as to why I didn't have as many friends as I used to. Though in reality I did have many friends, but because of the way I would interact with them I did not view them as a friend. Confusing, I know, so put yourself in my shoes.

Will knew everyone's name as they entered the club. The best part was he knew something about them, whether a spouse's name or what they enjoyed doing. Will would always have crazy stories. One time he tried to convince his small Toyota it was a Hummer so it could get over a wall of snow and make it to the gym on time only to get stuck on an "island" of snow. He explained how his wheels spun as the car's front axle was up in the air. Will brought his friendly—North Carolinian, hip-African American mentality to New England and spread joy every day amongst the community. The gym members loved him. Thanks to Will's influence, the old me started to come back. I began to embrace everyone I came in contact with at the club and outside of it. It felt great to be reminded that this was the way to treat people.

Everyone who works at Orchard Hills are nice people. Without Marcia I would have never gotten my job at Orchard. When she heard there was an opening she immediately thought of me. She is one of the best people I know. Cindy, Denise, Barbara, Carla everyone in management to personal trainers (especially Scott and Ben, who took me under their wing to make sure I was well educated in personal training) to swimming instructors (Paula and Sandy especially) were awesome and referred to me as their "boy toy".

Joe the maintenance guy, nicknamed me "Zap." Why, I don't know. I thought it was kind of catchy. Jeff, the massage therapist and yoga instructor wanted me to take one of his hot yoga classes for free just to experience it. And there was Ray. Ray was new at Orchard Hills. He was the kind of guy who instead of killing a bug to get rid of it would pick it up and take it outside. This one time a raccoon got into a barrel outside of the club and Ray refused to be the one who called animal control because he said they would kill it.

All these people already cared about me more than people I knew for four years at UMass. This was the type of atmosphere I wanted to work in. This atmosphere of friendliness is how the world should be, but there's a lot of people out there only concerned with themselves.

One of the best parts, if not the best aspect of my new life, was that I hardly ever thought of the accident in a negative way. For example, instead going into the gym and not being able to conduct exercises correctly or not see results, I was seeing results doing exercises I know I could do. This translated to real-life situations. No more losing my balance when I would try to step over something, no more hurting myself.

During my senior year of high school, after the accident, at my friend Gaetanno's we decided to go sledding. His house is located off a large hill. The paved ground was covered by a light snow. Gaetanno, Matt, and Travis all sled down the street with success. It was my turn. I ran as fast as I could and did a big belly flop on the board and sled halfway down the hill. I did not go as far as the other guys, and I also noticed that my left hand hurt extremely bad. My hand was covered in blood when I stood. I had slid on my hand the whole way down the hill. My brain told me to pick up the right hand, but because I had not completely gotten rid of my left side neglect, my brain forgot to tell the left hand to get off the ground. I laughed because that's how I dealt with these kinds of situations. I'd make fun of myself to make the pain go away, to fit in. But in reality, it hurt, a lot! But now there was no more of this, no more hurting myself due to my injury. I just had to make sure I was in control, focused, on what I was doing.

I started to notice that when I was on Facebook I would look at other people's pages, pictures, statuses, etc., and I would wish that I was there or I was involved in that. I In reality it didn't matter what anyone else was doing because it wasn't mylife. I had so much to accomplish and couldn't let wishing I was somewhere else get in the way because guess what? I'm not anywhere else, I'm here. I had to make the here and now worth it and get done what I had to do. So I stopped hanging out so much on Facebook. I heard a good quote that says, "It's not the desTonition, but the journey." This couldn't be truer to bring happiness. It did not matter if I moved to

Florida, L.A., South Carolina or wherever. I was in Massachusetts so why not make my time living in Mass., worth it.

In my free time at work in the fitness center I would study for my personal training test. I wanted to take the test as soon as I could and start training. I wanted to take the test before I graduated college. This way I could get my degree and start my life completely fresh. I had everything lined up that I wanted to accomplish. Because I was studying to be a personal trainer I realized I must do cardio and have the proper nutrition in my diet. I started eating healthy and running a mile before every workout. My logic was I had to practice what I preached or no one would take my advice. I had been hesitant to run before my workouts because it took so much work to concentrate on where my left foot was going to land. I would be exhausted even before my workouts.

When I started running a mile before my workouts, my form improved much more than it was previously. No more would my left leg flail away from my body and land on the plastic exterior of the treadmill, no more would I fall off and embarrass myself in front of strangers. My legs were finally strong enough to carry my body weight the distance of a mile without any problems.

I then realized perhaps my greatest joy. I was so much happier incorporating baseball in my life. I started to integrate it in my life, daily. I would follow the Red Sox avidly. I would root them on with passion. I wasn't hoping to play baseball anymore and was able to recognize and understand it was just a form of entertainment. I decided to embrace it, not ignore it's existence. Don't get me wrong, I still have hopes of running on that field again, but I had bigger shoes to fill. I had to help others. It didn't help however, that the Sox started 0-6 in 2011!!

During my Internship I met a nice lady named Carol. As I cleaned the stationary bikes in the spin room one day, I looked at Carol as she said, "There's something about you. I used to be a nurse and . . . there's just something." I explained my story and told her about the journey to recovery I was on for several years. She exclaimed, "I knew there was something!" I told her that I was writing a book about my experience, about my journey, and I hoped to one day be able to work with people rehabbing from brain injuries. She loved the idea and told me that she had a friend that conducted writing seminars. Her name was Gal but her nickname was "Pooh" or "Nushka" (I still don't know what to call her). Carol told me that she was going to set up a meeting for me.

Immediately following my internship one Wednesday afternoon, Gail met me at Orchard Hills. She came with a ton of information for me to look over while she read the synopsis and the first chapter. A half an hour went by and she came out to get a coffee. She told me how good of a recovery I had made, got our coffee (she bought me one), and went back into the conference room. We talked about everything I wanted for my book, the potential my book had, and we talked about an editor that she wanted to set me up with. The only problem was he lived in Kentucky. I told her I wasn't sure if I would financially be able to go. She said, "Well, I'll talk to Carol and we'll see what we can do." Astonished that she semi-offered to pay for my plane ticket, we kept on talking about my book and the possibly journeys I could take to get it published. I walked her to the exit and she offered me a hand shake and said, "It was a pleasure working with you", I responded with "It was great working with you too." Then, before she let go of my hand she asked, "Can I have a hug?" I said, "Of course" and gave her a hug and watched her walk out into the parking lot.

The same day I met Gail, I watched a boxing class at my gym. When I got home from that I checked my email. I had an email from California, a person whose mother had been in a car accident and suffered a traumatic brain injury in India. She wrote asking for tips to help her mother rehab her right side and to help her speech. I told her she should use her right hand for everything and she should sing to exercise her vocal cords. I went on with other ideas and suggestions for the life that day by day, year by year, she would have relearn. I really truly believe that this was why God saved me. To help others with this injury. I always knew there was a reason. I think I finally found it.

As my final semester came to a close, I still studied hard for my personal training certification. On all the practice questions I did extremely well. No matter what I read I knew the information before I would actually get to it in the text. Finally, I had it with studying. It seemed I knew everything I was reading. I said to myself, "This is stupid, I'm just going to take it tomorrow."

I started the multiple choice that night I got home from work. The following day I spent 10 straight hours looking at a computer screen taking the test. I'd decided I would not take this test again; I would pass it my first time. The test had a sixty percent passing rate.

I did not finish the test that Saturday. It was online so it didn't matter. I could take my time. I did two questions on Sunday, then finished the exam after four more questions on Monday. I submitted it. Later that night I remembered ISSA was located in California, three hours behind. My test might have been corrected already. I checked my email.

It read: **"ISSA CFT Exam final pass 87% . . . Congratulations well done!"**

I had done it! I could finally start my career!

As graduation came, I had no feelings. I felt like it was just something that I had to attend and get it over with. Everyone else in my graduating class were all excited that they were graduating. As they should be it is a very important milestone, great accomplishment. But for me this wasn't the greatest thing I had accomplished. When everyone else was worried if they would graduate or not, I was worried if I was going to be normal.

A few weeks passed and May 14th, 2011 came. The day that very few thought would come for me. I was going to graduate from the University of Massachusetts Amherst with a degree in journalism and a minor in political science. Many had their doubts, but I had proved the doubters and haters wrong again. Around 1:00 pm the journalism majors lined up to receive our medals for graduating. When they called our names they projected our faces on a large screen behind us. I thought to myself *I got to go out with a bang*. When they called my name, my image was projected on the screen. I turned my head and pretended to pick my nose. With everyone in attendance laughing, I walked up to the women who would give me my medal. I shook her hand, grabbed my medal, thanked God and walked off the stage to complete the next task many people will also doubt I can accomplish.

REFLECTION

A lot of people think I am cocky or what have you. People can think I'm cocky. I don't care because I am actually just extremely proud of everything I have accomplished only 22 years into this life. I have survived something many said I would not. Doctors said if I did survive I would not be able to live a normal life, I would be a vegetable. Yet, I graduated from a University in four years and added a personal training certification. I have saved lives. I have helped make a better quality of life for those dealing with a brain injury. I inspired people to return to their faith. I have written a book about my trials hoping it will inspire and lead others in a positive direction. How could I not feel pride in my accomplishments? I still have dreams of playing baseball and going pro. I'm not sure why I still have these fantasies after all the times I've talked myself out of it, but I do. Every time I see a ball game or see the sport I used to be obsessed with, images of me running through the outfield fill my head; I still believe that one day I will get the chance to play baseball professional but I am not obsessed with the idea like was. Now I am able to suppress those emotions and concentrate on whatever it is that I am currently doing.

I still struggle dribbling a basketball. I still love women. I still love different cultures and love the act of learning about these things. I do love these things, but I am ready to move on with my life with them or without them knowing down the road these aspects of life will be waiting. I still at times think like a girl (care to much about certain things). But the difference is that now I am able to stop and think about the situation before I act upon my feelings. I'll get mad then stop, consider, and say to myself "Wait, I don't actually care."

I'm actually glad the accident happened.

This must be weird to hear after reading all I have been through, but it's true. My role in life is obvious. What I need to do is clear; I am here to help people. God has given me a gift. I am also happy the accident happened because now I am a better person than I was before the accident. Before, I was an alcoholic who thought he was invincible. Who thought he could live life on the edge and nothing bad would ever happen. But now I am well educated on how stupidity and arrogance can lead to poor decisions.

I have seen the lowest of the lows that most people could not begin to understand. I have always been a tough person, but this experience has made me one of the toughest. Because of this ordeal I had to stop caring about what people thought about me. Even if they were staring at me, I had to do what was best for me. Whether it was running, walking, or asking what to others might seem stupid questions, I had to do it.

I know now nothing is too hard, that I can accomplish anything. If it had not been for my training for Div I baseball I probably would not have recovered to where I am today. Baseball made me work so much harder. I hate to say this, but at the time baseball was the only reason I went to college. I hated school, well, school work. I wanted to go to college to get a degree, but the thought of being able to play division one baseball was my main motivation. Because baseball made me go to college I was able to challenge my mind more than I would have if I hadn't attended college. The challenge helped my brain recover greatly.

I have always been a hard worker, but I am not sure I would have been able to work as hard as I did working toward the goal of playing baseball. The thought kept me working day in and day out. I pushed myself until I realized I probably would never play baseball at the same level I was once able to.

I wrote in my book that I wished I had found these Facebook groups so I could find other people with my injury as I was going through the toughest part of my recovery. Looking back on it, I'm glad I didn't. I would have noticed how you were 'supposed' to end up with at the end of your recovery; speech problems and problems with mobility. This would have ruined my ignorance is bliss attitude.

I was so lonely all the time. I tried to figure out where I fit in. I thought that I was an outcast even though I had a ton of friends. Instead of finding out who I truly am, I tried to create who I was.

Thinking that I needed:

To be a division one athlete to fit in

An exotic girl

The perfect body

A girl because all my friends/ people I knew had one

Because I was trying to fit in I didn't have a normal, fun, awesome college experience. Instead of drinking and parties, I tooknaps and went to the gym. I grew up faster than most, I had to. I had to figure out what was important in life, what really mattered. My well being and my health came first, before drinking and hooking up with random girls. When I healed enough to go out and have a drink or two, Jon needed my help. Sure, he would have been fine on his own, but with my help it was a lot less stressful and he didn't have to worry.

One of the biggest things I learned that with a brain injury; you cannot dwell on what you don't have or what you used to have. I wouldn't let myself move beyond the past for the longest time. I discovered that you cannot do this. I had to take what I did have and move on with my life. As soon as I did that I was able to be truly happy again.

I'm never going to play division one baseball as I'd dreamed every day of my young adult life, but I don't care. God has something better for me. He wants me to help people who have these types of injuries, he wants me to give people hope. I now know why God saved me that night. I have a purpose in life. I will fulfill the duties that have been bestowed upon me.

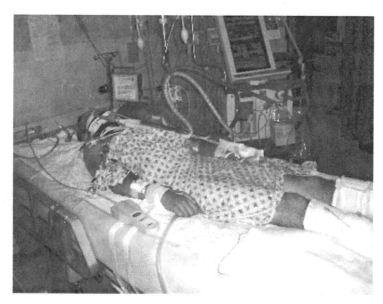

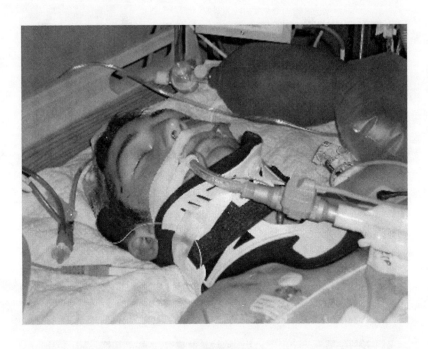

CPSIA information can be obtained at www.ICGtesting.com
Printed in the USA
LVOW041852270312

275003LV00005B/155/P